# Discla

The LinkedIn Rockstars are third party professionals focused on the LinkedIn platform. We are not in any way associated with LinkedIn. Rather, we work independently to support the user community

# RockTheWorld with LinkedIn v2.1

Co-authored by Mike O'Neil & Lori Ruff, "The LinkedIn Rockstars"
Layout and Design by Andrew Cameron

*www.IntegratedAlliances.com*

promotions@IntegratedAlliances.com

**Integrated Alliances**
P.O. Box, 968
Prior Lake, MN 55372

ISBN 978-0-9862417-0-3 Print Book

ISBN 978-0-9862417-1-0 eBook

1. Business Strategy 2. LinkedIn 3. Social Media

4. Sales Training 5. Social Networking

# Sign up for Free

## eCopy Updates to

## Rock The World

## with LinkedIn at

www.RockTheWorldFan.com

Rock on,

# Part of a Plan

RockTheWorld with LinkedIn is a component in the Integrated Alliances world-class LinkedIn and Social Selling programs.

Dating back to 2006 when Mike O'Neil delivered the world's first-ever LinkedIn training, this material has always has a rock and roll element and style to it. For example:

1. Students are greeted by classic rock as they enter the "classroom", usually the Eagles, Pink Floyd or Kid Rock.

2. A record album has about 12 songs on it. The training classes have about that many topics in them. It's a familiar formula and audiences really like it, especially in shorter sessions, like a 1-hour keynote or breakout or in a webinar.

   An afternoon workshop is more intensive, like a series of albums or even double albums (e.g. Frampton Comes Alive!). The material is carefully layered so it is very easy for sales teams that always have customers on their minds, even when they are in a training class.

3. Songs are about 3-4 minutes in length and each topic is about that long. Then comes a little Q&A. This is the typical attention span of a sales rep on a single topic and we model our programs after it to make it super-easy for them to follow, to get involved and to implement what they learn.

It is the power of rock music' LinkedIn and Social Selling that makes this book, this material and Integrated Alliances so powerful TOGETHER.

For this reason, we have incorporated an amazing SOUNDTRACK to make RockTheWorld with LinkedIn even more interesting for readers and "listeners." The soundtrack can be found throughout the book, in summary form at the end of this book in the SoundTrack Set List as well as online at www.RockTheWorldBook.com/music.

## Contact Us

Find out about Integrated Alliances at www.IntegratedAlliances.com, call 303-683-9600 or email Training@IntegratedAlliances.com. We will have your team climbing to the top of the sales charts in no time!

# Table of Contents

# APPENDIX ...... **137**

# Foreword with David Fishof

**CEO, Rock 'n' Roll Fantasy Camp**
**Rock Tour Producer & Promoter**
**Author "Rock Your Business"**

David Fishof has lived at the center of the music business for more than 25 years. Some of his biggest triumphs include reuniting The Monkees, pairing Roger Daltrey with The British Rock Symphony, and creating Ringo Starr's All-Star Band.

Fast forward to today and he is founder and CEO of Rock 'n' Roll Fantasy Camp with friends/celebrity counselors including Roger Daltrey of The Who, Brett Michaels of Poison, Tommy Lee of Motley Crüe, Gene Simmons and Paul Stanley of KISS, and hundreds more.

Throughout his innovative career, David learned from leading minds in the rock music business and wrapped it all up in a spot-on business book: **Rock Your Business**. In the book, David shares lessons learned and how they apply to your business challenges.

Mike bought one of the first copies and soon discovered two things.

♦ He had already been implementing several tips
♦ There were many more ideas he could use

Specifically, David preaches prototyping your solution, creating HYPE around it, pre-selling tickets, and bartering for things you need.

If you want a real advantage with fun and simple things you can really do, then Rock Your Business will help! (The book is available at *http://bit.ly/ROCKURBIZ*)

## The Rock 'n' Roll Fantasy Camp Connection

It started with a LinkedIn keyword search by Geno Orphanopoulos. He is from Rock 'n' Roll Fantasy Camp and is a veteran LinkedIn user. Fast forward 6 months to November 2010 and Mike O'Neil is attending Rock 'n' Roll Fantasy Camp with 50 other amateur musicians.

This amazing program is for musicians of all skill levels (from beginners to seasoned professionals), and all rock instruments (bass, drums, keyboards, harmonica, sax). Singers are invited and encouraged.

The camp Mike attended was held in San Francisco. After 3 days of rehearsals in a padded up hotel, it ended with each band playing 3 songs on stage at the Fillmore West on a Sunday evening.

Mike's band mates included a chiropractor, a medical equipment sales rep, a retired postal worker and the owner of the hotel that hosted the rehearsals. The band was named "Malpractice" and it fit!

Mike performed with his band of 5 "campers" and one true rockstar (Sandy Gennaro who played with Joan Jett & the Black Hearts, The Pat Travers Band, The Monkees and Cyndi Lauper).

Mike and David met at camp and their relationship grew. David shared how Rock 'n' Roll Fantasy Camp offered corporate events (and he went on to complete his book entitled Rock Your Business). One year later Mike O'Neil & Lori Ruff neared completion on the next release of RockTheWorld with LinkedIn v2.1 and the connection seemed unavoidable. This is the result.

To see Mike perform at Rock 'n' Roll Fantasy Camp, visit YouTube and search on _"Mike O'Neil Fantasy Camp"_. This search also leads to a great set of videos about promoting your events on LinkedIn, Twitter, EventBrite, Facebook and others.

## From David Himself

Mike joined us for the San Francisco Rock 'n' Roll Fantasy Camp in late 2010 that featured Dickey Betts of the Allman Brothers Band and a dozen famous (and not so famous) rock stars.

Mike had done some homework and knew about my rock tour background. I remember seeing him in a British Rock Symphony t-shirt on performance night. That tour is one of my favorites and it led to my strong relationship with Roger Daltrey, who sang the vocals on that tour. It's a rare thing to see that "T" 20 years later and it stuck with me. It turns out Mike had been to my Monkees and Ringo Starr tours as well.

We had longtime Rockstars in this camp so it was a reunion of sorts. Many Rockstars live in and around San Francisco, so it's easier for them to get involved. For example, this camp experienced Jack Blades of Night Ranger dropping by.

Once again, our big fan Ed Oates was in camp. Ed is the co-founder of Oracle (along with Larry Ellison). Ed plays a wicked guitar and he has attended nearly every camp we've held. Ed also wrote the forward to "Rock Your Business".

Mike approached me about contributing to his book. The title alone grabbed my interest and it seemed like our audiences were similar, which was good for each of us. I discuss partnerships in my book and this is in keeping with that principle.

He asked if I might summarize some of the cross-overs that business people might experience between the Rock 'n' Roll Fantasy Camp experience and business in general. This short list may generate additional ideas to help you "explore the space".

## Some of the biggies:

- ♦ A band resembles a workgroup or a management team. All must learn to sing from the same sheet of music: THE MISSION STATEMENT
- ♦ Everyone must agree on which songs to play and commit to learn them well: GOALS
- ♦ Someone ultimately determines who will play which parts of each song: MANAGERS and DECISION MAKERS
- ♦ The Rockstar is the supreme leader of the band: EXECUTIVE MANAGEMENT
- ♦ Song and performance ideas are encouraged, presented, tried, adapted, selected or rejected: PRODUCT DEVELOPMENT
- ♦ The fixed deadline can't be moved, the show goes live at 8pm: PROJECT DUE DATES

I am sure you will enjoy the rest of this book as it helps you become a rockstar in your line of business. I invite YOU to come have the time of your life at a Rock 'n' Roll Fantasy Camp (www.rockcamp.com). I'd love to meet you and help you Rock Your Business!

# Before we bring on the band...

## ...Let's set the stage:

RockTheWorld with LinkedIn is more ANALOG than DIGITAL. It helps baby boomers who remember vinyl records, MTV, the Sony Walkman and the Polaroid camera. It helps classic rock music fans, especially those that enjoy a live concert experience.

The book is sprinkled with over 50 classic rock tunes that queue up important topics. These principles help you better understand LinkedIn.

It's about Taking Care of Business. We will Show You The Way. We'll teach you how to Shout It Out Loud. You get the idea.

Many of the songs incorporated in the book are part of Mike's vinyl collection, many dating back to the 1970's when he got his FIRST turntable and stereo (both Technics).

Mike bought this Bang & Olufson turntable in college (1978) and he still has it today. It gets used often! Mike visits the Electric Fetus used record store every month or two to look for new (old) vinyl to feed the B&O and feed his mind!

## THIS BOOK IS DIFFERENT

RockTheWorld with LinkedIn features a REAL music video soundtrack showing the bands performing these songs (thanks to YouTube). We think it makes the learning process a little more fun so you are a little more inspired to follow through. Think about the Saturday Night Fever and how that soundtrack set the tone. This book picks up on that a little bit here.

We incorporate a wide variety of videos:

♦ Concert versions from "back then"
♦ Current concert footage of these old time bands
♦ Original MTV-style videos TV show appearances – Soul Train, Letterman

We hope you enjoy this new approach to learning LinkedIn while having fun!

**TIP**

Throughout the book you will find a series of useful TIPs. They are a sprinkling of best practices and strategies to save you time and increase your effectiveness. The LinkedIn Rockstars developed these methodologies over a period of 8+ years of active use, training and consulting.

**TIP**

Twin Browser Sessions. When crafting your Profile online, have TWO browser TABs open - one in the Edit Mode and the other in View Mode. It helps in checking your work. Use them both, back and forth, to save a little time.

# Why we write about LinkedIn

**We feel it is important to write about what you know: for us, that's LinkedIn for business and classic rock music for inspiration! After all, shouldn't business be fun? We think so.**

Mike is from the corporate world, where he had quotas, cubes, company-supplied computers (starting with dual floppies) and access to computer databases like Computer Intelligence (now Harte-Hanks), Hoovers and the like. Mike even experienced RIF's (layoffs) - twice.

Lori hails from the corporate HR and training world, where credentials are everything. It's a world of resumes, CV's, background checks and endless end-user training.

*The historic Hayes 1200 Modem; Mike had one just like it!*

That said, "you go with what you know" and we know LinkedIn for business very well. This book is our way of bottling up some of what we have learned from our real world experiences and merging it with inspiration in the form of some some excellent classic rock music.

LinkedIn in the 21st century really is old school. In many ways, it's a modern day version of the Hoovers-type database services, which themselves are more akin to the Bulletin Board Systems (BBS) where we used "squeally" modems to dial up to the Internet a little faster every few years from 300, 1200bps, 14.4k, even 56k. That old data-driven mentality, with minimal graphics, is much like LinkedIn even to this day.

LinkedIn depends on words more than pictures. This makes it easy to read and to hone in on important business information.

_"Still Crazy After All These Years"_ (Paul Simon, 1977) describes how we prefer simple-to-understand and simple-to-use systems like LinkedIn. Is that so crazy? The Facebook world of hidden menus, photos, likes, etc. is much less appealing to us, especially for fast-paced business.

LinkedIn is integrating more and more with the likes of SalesForce.com and Hoovers all the time. In a nutshell, LinkedIn is 1) free for most people and 2) has the people you want to reach. That says it all, doesn't it?

# Chapter One

## The PURPOSE of Your LinkedIn Profile

Learn why LinkedIn is so important as we get you in the right frame of mind. Learn about the role your LinkedIn profile plays and how to use it to "back you up" in business. A simple and logical LinkedIn Business Methodology gives you a step-by-step roadmap to follow."

When Mike joined LinkedIn on January 14, 2004, "Why LinkedIn?" was a really good question. Still, Mike trained over a dozen individuals that year. When Mike started to deliver LinkedIn training to businesses and associations in 2006, LinkedIn still wasn't a clear leader in the mostly unknown industry known as Social Media. Mike delivered over 50 LinkedIn group trainings that year.

The LinkedIn IPO had a huge positive impact, opening the eyes of companies, employees and especially executives. LinkedIn is now one of the big boys, along-side Amazon, Apple, Hoovers and SalesForce.com.

Recruiters, once enchanted with Monster and CareerBuilder, switched to LinkedIn long ago. Many recruiters pay $500 a month or more for LinkedIn and happy as heck to do so. Job seeking has been turned upside down.

At this point, there's _"No Lookin' Back"_ (Michael McDonald, 1985). This is the way it's going to be; so strap in for a Rockin' Ride!

Tools of the trade change over time. Tools such as the FAX, copier, modem, file servers, mainframes, offices, conference rooms, even the phone...

The tools of the trade circa 2012 have a lot to do with WHERE you are. Offices are replaced by a spare bedroom at home. Meetings are virtual or at Starbucks. There might not even be an office anymore!

Here's what it might look like now. Does this sound familiar?

**Mechanical tools:**

- A tricked out home office setup with a Voice Over IP (VOIP) phone, high speed Internet (cable or DSL), Cisco WiFi Router, big external flat panel monitor, 1Gb external USB hard disk from Best Buy.
- Windows laptop or a MacBookPro with a big hard drive that still runs out of space and loads of memory that still isn't enough.
- Microsoft Office (Word, Excel, PowerPoint, Outlook), even on a Mac.
- Multiple browsers, especially Firefox, Chrome, IE (PC only), Safari.
- Backup system just in case, perhaps Internet-based and/or local.
- SmartPhone like an iPhone, Android, Blackberry (well, maybe not).
- For a growing number, more computing devices than humans in the house!

## Social and online tools:

- Active LinkedIn Account, Profile, Network
- Twitter account – even if you don't use it much
- Facebook account – wanting it for personal use, but crossing over
- Business card with address, cell phone, email address, LinkedIn profile URL

Are you surprised when someone is NOT on LinkedIn nowadays? Do you think they are missing something? Do you feel less confident about their judgment?

## We've heard it before, haven't we?

- Oh, that Internet thing will blow over, just give it a little time
- An Email address? They know how to reach me
- A Web site? We do business in person, not over dial up modems

# LinkedIn Users Rock in Business

**LinkedIn users are business leaders who want to do business with people like you.**

When LinkedIn users are put in a room together, they often feel an instant connection with one another for a number of reasons. Demographics are key. The make-up of the LinkedIn user community is business people - pure and simple. That said, LinkedIn users automatically have one thing in common, don't they? LinkedIn!

Want to strike up a conversation at an event? There is something good to strike up a business conversation about!

It is the PEOPLE that make LinkedIn, well, LinkedIn! LinkedIn is for *"Taking Care of Business"* (Bachman Turner Overdrive, 1976) and the pace of growth is accelerating. It is not LinkedIn itself, but rather LinkedIn users that are the prize.

Why trust the LinkedIn Rockstars? Individually and together, we've trained over 500 business audiences since early 2006. We were BOTH named to the Forbes Top 50 Social Media Power Influencers List (#21 and #25), a list topped by the likes of Chris Brogan, Guy Kawasaki, Brian Solis and several people we actually trained years ago.

*"The Heart of the Matter"* (Don Henley, 1989) is that LinkedIn has the best user community for B2B business activity. It is highly populated with business decision-makers, executives, business owners, financiers, recruiters, HR professionals, technologists, sales and marketing professionals, coaches and consultants and much more.

While LinkedIn began in the San Francisco Bay area, it quickly spread to other large cities around the United States and around the world. The other heavy pockets of users are in the Northeast U.S. (New York, Boston, etc.), the UK, the Netherlands and India.

Because LinkedIn is a web-based community (cloud-based, SaaS, PaaS), individuals in very small towns can be fully engaged with others in their profession and out. LinkedIn levels the playing field.

# The Exponential Power of LinkedIn

**Online relationships have capabilities that far exceed traditional relationships – the power to Click, Forward, Share, Like! Learn how to embrace and leverage that power.**

This chart may help you understand the power of a LinkedIn network. If you were directly connected to 10 people and if each were connected to 10 more people and so on, you'd have over 1,000 in your extended (3-tier) network.

*Others* $\quad 2 \times 10 = 20$

Linked**in**. $\quad 2^{10} \quad = 1024$

*The exponential power of the LinkedIn 3-tier network*

Today, more and more business relationships start online. In fact, Mike and Lori met on LinkedIn and look what happened! It is a similar story in many of our significant business relationships at this point in the game. DO you have significant business or personal relationships that started online?

As you get more involved online, notice how "strangers" become friends and partners, all because of a chance meeting online.

Many relationships STAY online for a very long time, perhaps indefinitely; even relationships among customers, partners and vendors. This is amplified even more when we begin talking about international operations, outsourcing, distributed workforces, etc.

The power of business introductions, whether formal or informal, takes on much more meaning when you have accurate and current information about the person you want to engage. You can "do your homework" today with little effort.

It all happens because of your LinkedIn Profile. The more people who build out their LinkedIn profiles, the richer the environment is for everyone in the LinkedIn community.

# Your LinkedIn Profile Makes YOU the Star!

**On LinkedIn, you are defined by your words, by your profile. It represents you to the business world in a super-interactive way; one that allows others to interact with you with minimal effort.**

Your LinkedIn Profile answers the question *"Who Are You?"* (The Who, 1973) from a businessperson's perspective. It is a compilation of business-related information sprinkled with select personal elements that paint a sort of 3D portrait of what you are like to do business with, what you are like to be around.

Your profile shows viewers what makes you special. It lets you introduce yourself to people you'd never meet. Make it a dynamic portrait of the real you.

A spiffin' LinkedIn Profile is a live album, where an "average" LinkedIn Profile is more of a studio album (and not a great studio album at that). Which one paints a better picture of the band?

## Your Identity

Your LinkedIn Profile is your identity on LinkedIn. Where a company has an online presence, so does an individual.

An individual has a LinkedIn Profile and it works as a detailed record of your career, capabilities, and interests. If that sounds like an online resume, you are not too far off base. Your LinkedIn profile puts you in the driver's seat for your "Online Reputation."

A LinkedIn Profile replaces Monster.com, CareerBuilder.com and HotJobs.com for job seekers nowadays.

The (rapidly declining) number of people using these services is composed almost exclusively of job seekers, recruiters and HR professionals. There is no business development activity here.

Although there are many recruiters and job seekers successfully using LinkedIn, for the most part, users are gainfully employed. This is a tool they use IN their business and FOR their business.

Think of it this way – your LinkedIn Profile is there to help you in two ways: to Attract Opportunities and to Find Opportunities. People, for the most part, are on LinkedIn to be FOUND – found by people they WANT to be found by.

**A properly formulated LinkedIn Profile is a combination of the following:**

### Your Online Professional Biography

A mini-website all about you. A bio is about why you are significant, important, and/or qualified to do what you do. It lists your accomplishments. That's your LinkedIn Profile.

It should agree with your resume and can, in fact, even "replace" your resume in some instances.

### Your Resume

Your LinkedIn Profile shows your work history, skills, education, etc. as including a really nice summary for readers. It serves as a "2012-era resume" in a growing number of professional circles.

**TIP**

**Looking for work?**

Never indicate loudly that you are unemployed. Don't say you are "Unemployed at Unemployed!" Hiring managers and recruiters are looking for people with skills and abilities that match the requirements of the job they need to fill, not someone defined as "unemployed."

Use care when completing your profile to identify the skills and knowledge and other attributes you possess that show why you are the best person for the position they need to fill.

### Your Personal Web Page

Your LinkedIn Profile has information about your business that is often found on a web page. In fact, LinkedIn even lets you insert links to your web page (up to three actually).

### Your Online Advertisement

Your LinkedIn Profile tells people what you can do for them: your skills, your capabilities, your offerings. It tells them why you are in this business space, how others can help you and what you have to offer that they might need.

## Your Future

Where a resume looks about 90% backward and 10% forward, your LinkedIn Profile is at least 50% forward-looking. This is especially true for the Summary section of your LinkedIn Profile.

## Your Interests

People like to see more about a person than all business. They like to know more about you, the person. LinkedIn makes it easy to do this, and it even has some very useful tools for you to find others with the same interests.

## TIP

Don't overlook the power of personal and professional Interests when developing your LinkedIn Profile. People do business with people they know and trust. Trust is built first on shared experience. This is where you have a real opportunity to connect to people with whom you have common interests. Even if they do not need your services at the moment, they might open doors to help connect you to people who do!

## What a LinkedIn Profile is NOT

It is NOT your life, your picture(s), your favorite songs, your friends, or a collection of insignificant information about you. It is a business and not a pure social tool. Facebook does a very good job in the more social areas.

## Purpose of the LinkedIn Profile

Your LinkedIn Profile serves many purposes, but the biggest is to help you to be found and to give you professional credibility.

Your LinkedIn Profile should be part of a larger attraction strategy. Keep in mind your profile is not static; once you write it you will want to check it periodically to keep it fresh and relevant to maximize your personal brand.

# What NOT to do on Your LinkedIn Profile

**Your zipper is open; there is food on your face; a bad online presence can have the same effect – turning people off. Yet you may never even know why there is little response to your efforts.**

It's the call that never happens, the viewer that quickly clicks away, you know, the one who hits the "Back" button after those magical 3-5 seconds convince them they are looking at the wrong profile. Your online presence can just as easily REPEL the business you are trying to attract.

If you've been on LinkedIn for a while and haven't seen stellar results you hear from others, it might be your profile. In fact, a bad profile can turn a deal around and send them to a competitor.

*"I can't go for that"* (Hall and Oates, 1981)

## Reasons your profile repels others

- ♦ Looks like you're seeking a job and are not. OK if you are, not OK if you are in sales, a business owner, etc. For goodness sakes, do it with style. Don't say "Unemployed at Unemployed" as your Headline or list it as a job for example.
- ♦ No picture or bad picture. Shows you "don't get it" or "can't figure it out" and raises suspicions that you have other shortcomings as well.
- ♦ Too few connections. Is it that nobody likes you, you don't have any people to connect to or you're keeping your circle really tight. It raises suspicions that you're either unpopular or overly shy. Everyone should have at least a modest network size (500 is a minimum). A dozen connections will NOT do for building any respect on LinkedIn, neither will 100.
- ♦ Misspppellingz can kill a relationship VERY fast, especially if they are not hidden in LOTS of text.

## A Worst Practice Parading as a Best Practice

Seen a LinkedIn Profile that sounds like a documentary – "Mr. Thomas" is this and "Ms. Johnson" is that? It's called 3rd person and it HAS NO PLACE IN LINKEDIN PROFILES.

You're a person, not a product. Your LinkedIn Profile is a dialogue between you and the reader.

It is NOT a list of facts about you. It is NOT a story about you. It is a narrative told BY you to others. It's what you share at a business networking event, over a beer.

How do those conversations go?

- ♦ What is your value statement to your target audience?
- ♦ What do people typically ask you about who you are and what you do?
- ♦ What do you say to people about you "as a person?"
- ♦ What is your call to action? When and how should people reach out to you?

There are lots of variations and styles but your profile, and especially your Summary, is a message FROM you and not a story ABOUT you.

So, read your profile aloud with a critical ear asking yourself "If the perfect person for me to meet were standing right in front of me, what would I say to them".

# LinkedIn Helps You "Back It Up"

**Credentials mean everything in business today, especially in a virtual world and LinkedIn is perhaps the best "credentialing" tool for individuals and businesses alike!**

Sooner or later, everyone is expected to make a claim and "back it up", be it in sales, marketing, interviews - you name it.

There are two components to backing it up, both are supported by LinkedIn.

The way to "Back It Up" is your profile, which contains your personal credentials. This book focuses on presenting your credentials to build trust and credibility in this online world.

The second way to "Back It Up" is your activity on LinkedIn. Do respectable things and get respected. It's the Pay It Forward principle.

Look at _www.RockTheWorldBook.com_ for the latest help to improve your overall success on LinkedIn. Remember that, once your profile is Rockstar grade, they will find you and engage you. BE READY AND RESPOND!

## Audiences

Different people look at your profile for different reasons. While your profile has a primary audience (your perfect customer, you might say), it has secondary audiences as well. This is especially true if you are open to new opportunities, new partners or new customers. Still, your primary audience comes first.

Example: we primarily serve larger corporate sales teams and small and medium sized firms where "everyone is a sales person." Our language is focused there, but it has feelers to our secondary audiences that include recruiting, marketing, engineering and the like.

## The Numbers

There is no way around it, you will be comparing numbers in the LinkedIn world and the bigger number usually wins. A _platinum_ selling record is usually better than a _hit_ record is better than just a record, at least from a business perspective (and we focus on business).

Let LinkedIn's "Profile Completeness" statistic prod you along and incent you to build out your profile. Funny thing – you are the only one who can see this.

A score of 100%, while technically complete, does not give you a Rockstar-Grade profile. Don't worry though, by the time you finish this book, you'll know how.

## Other Ways to "Back It Up"

Work Experiences give you ammunition to "Back It Up" as well. For some, Education is where they 'Back It Up." Organizations you support, projects completed, publications, they all add to the "Back It Up" mix.

LinkedIn Recommendations are a terrific way to 'Back It Up." Sure, the numbers can be padded here like elsewhere, but recommendations get results and more is better. Each recommendation is a VOTE for you and for your work.

We'll teach you to obtain recommendations that boost reader trust, credibility and make people want to do business with you.

The most obvious "Back It Up" number is your LinkedIn connections. With networks growing and growing, 500 connections aren't what they used to be.

Still, LinkedIn wants to round everybody down to 500+ in how they display statistics. To get credit for your entire network, you have to do a little extra.

## Where and how to "tell it"

We suggest telling others about your network size here:

- ◆ Headline, part of the 120 characters or
- ◆ Summary, part of 2,000 characters

Try language like "1,500 connections". Do not list any network statistics other than tier 1 connections. Do not say something like "15,000,000 Total Connections". Frankly, you can have 15,000,000 total connections with less than 10 direct connections. We know how.

# RockTheWorld™ LinkedIn Methodology

**Our time-tested, systematic approach to LinkedIn will help you avoid stepping in some really nasty LinkedIn and Social Media puddles.**

Since early 2006, we have trained B2B sales, recruiting and executive professionals to use LinkedIn and we've pretty much seen or tried it all.

We've discovered what works, what doesn't, tried different things, in different ways, in different orders, with different results. We've found the edge, gone over it, and are well equipped to show you what to do.

Because we've focused our training on LinkedIn for so long, we often feel like "masters of the obvious." The RockTheWorld LinkedIn Business Methodology seems so logical now.

This methodology seems logical now, but that wasn't always the case and not everyone knows about it. Have you seen anyone with an empty profile sending "Invitation to join my network" invitations to lots of people to connect? Doesn't work so well, does it?

Nowadays, it seems obvious, but that was not always the case. When Mike joined LinkedIn, you could upload 50,000 email addresses, over and over, and build your network quickly. LinkedIn put the brakes on it You are now limited to just 3,000 outbound invitations in your entire life.

Your success is dependent on following our methodology in the RIGHT ORDER. Remember Michael Jackson and the Jackson 5? *ABC, Easy as 1-2-3?* How would that sound as CAB, easy as 2-1-3? Sure, it still rhymes, but it wouldn't have been a chart-topper would it?

Want your profile to top the charts? This is your roadmap:

1. Get yourself a spiffin' LINKEDIN PROFILE, ready for business, one that acts as your proxy and invites your target market to reach out to you.
2. Build your LinkedIn NETWORK, but only after your profile is spiffin'. This fills your pond full of hungry fish that bite the bait on your hook. No profile or bad profile? No Bait!
3. Employ LinkedIn SEARCH tools to find the individuals you seek: those with whom you want to do business.
4. ENGAGE those that you believe might fit. Carefully use the LinkedIn communications options, but don't forget or ignore traditional methods (phone, Email). Now you are loaded with business intelligence to get further, faster.
5. BUSINESS. Sales professionals are off to find customers, channel managers are off engaging partners, individuals are off to find work... you get the idea.

# Chapter Two

## Getting Ready to Rock
## With Your LinkedIn Profile

Learn how to use the RockTheWorld book. It's a little bit different than many books you've experienced. Prepare for the process as you gather up what you will need (provisions) then learn about the profile development process. Learn about the components in your totally rockin' LinkedIn profile!

We wrote this "how-to" book to provide you with a SIMPLE system to build a powerful LinkedIn Presence. _"Show Me the Way"_ (Peter Frampton, 1973) said users and we responded with _RockTheWorld™_! It is a smooth combination of strategies, tactics and real screen shots with SIMPLE instructions.

We even outline two paths you may care to consider as you dive into your LinkedIn Profile. Don't think this book is just for beginners. We've packed plenty of extra material for experienced users interested in polishing their image..

_Training wheels done "LinkedIn Rockstar style." Mike actually drove a '69 Z-28 in High School._

Our LinkedIn Profile process is highly refined, road-tested and it brings immediate results. We've written hundreds of LinkedIn Profiles for clients, each with different roles, functional areas, levels of responsibility, and industries.

We have also written templates for teams, companies, and even groups and associations to standardize their language, enhance their credibility and build their brand.

After delivering hundreds of LinkedIn group training sessions for companies, groups and associations, we have optimized the use of LinkedIn as a business relationship-building and prospecting tool.

For best results don't go _"Helter Skelter"_ (The Beatles, 1966). Let the book guide you through the process. Give it "full play" then go back and listen to the song that rings most true for you. Follow the process for your first draft and THEN drill down and optimize the sections as you see fit.

Don't try to do too much at once. There is no point in getting overwhelmed and giving up before you give yourself a good chance at success!

Focus your time; do a little bit each day and soon you will have perfected your online reputation using LinkedIn.

Now, if the book really strikes your fancy...

# The LinkedIn Profile Crash Course

One reader described her "relationship with the (first edition of the) book" in a LinkedIn message to Mike.

It was a dreary weekend and Sara had just gotten the book from Amazon.com. She put the radio on a classic rock channel, had a cup of coffee and her laptop on the couch. Nice and comfy.

By the end of the day, she was ready to start showing off her early prototype profile to others. It was probably dozens of songs later and she was almost there. By Monday AM, her profile was spiffin' and she was off to the races. It was a "one person retreat."

### 10,000 ft. View of the LinkedIn Profile

To help you succeed, we provide a real overview, followed by an inspiring step-by-step process, to get you started properly down the path on LinkedIn.

We find it helps us to get a 10,000-foot view before landing on the ground to get the big picture, to know what to expect, and to understand the final goal.

We know your time is valuable and limited, so we focused the content of this book on the important things and occasionally, we'll point them out to you. This will help you focus your energies and get the best possible results.

Generally, the best process is:

1. Gather information to include in your LinkedIn Profile. Sources include Resume, Bio, CV, Website, company marketing materials. (See the next section for a more complete list.)
2. Fire up your word processing software: doesn't matter which.
3. Put your favorite classic rock station on the radio.
4. Follow the steps in the book to build out the various sections.
5. On LinkedIn, select "edit" your Profile then Copy/Paste the text from your word processing software into your LinkedIn Profile one section at a time. (DO NOT upload your resume to LinkedIn. Take our word for it!)
6. Select "view" your Profile and pay careful attention to its visual appearance. It's got to layout right to get the maximum effect.
7. Have a smart phone? Download the LinkedIn app and view your profile on the device. More and more, people will be viewing your profile on handheld devices.
8. Search for yourself by name (including alternate spellings) and a few select keywords to see how you rank. You might choose to modify some fields to improve your standings.

## Why not just type your profile right into LinkedIn?

Good question. There are a number of good reasons.

♦ The LinkedIn system has no spell check capability: spelling and grammar errors significantly hurt your credibility just as in a resume or a cover letter.
♦ LinkedIn often provides very small windows for entering text. In many cases, you can only see 20 or 50 characters and may be entering more than that.
♦ Have an offline backup in case you make a mistake and have to start over.
♦ This is a good starting point for your profile on other Social Media platforms.
♦ The word processing software gives you options to add special formatting characters and bullets that make your profile spring out from the screen. More on this later.

**TIP**

Use a browser that has spell checking. As of this writing that includes Mozilla Firefox or Google Chrome, but not Internet Explorer or Safari.

# Provisions For The journey

*"What you need"* (INXS, 1985)

**There are certain (electronic) documents and other data elements that you will want to have handy unless you really enjoy creative writing and exercising your fingertips!**

To make this journey successful, you will want to pack certain "provisions" to help you along the way; to assist you with the data collection part of creating your profile. Here is a simple checklist of things to gather up (in no particular order). It really helps to have electronic versions wherever possible, of course

### A resume or biography

- A portfolio of your work, especially for creative types
- A decent headshot photo
- Your blog URL
- Website addresses you want to include (up to 3)
- Articles you have written (if online, gather the links as well.)
- Profile language from other social networking sites
- Letters of recommendation
- Job Information about previous employers, including Websites
- Job titles, descriptions, and start/stop dates (years is usually fine)
- Significant volunteer experiences, including roles, responsibilities, start/stop dates (years is usually fine)
- Professional volunteer and Awards
- Professional Certifications
- A list of the full name (and associated ACRONYM) of the groups and associations you belong to, those related to your industry, or those related to the industries of your clients and vendors

Create a list of your professional and personal interests. Include community service interests and other things that make it appear you lead a balanced life.

Contact information – Web site URL, Phone #, Street Address or P.O. Box, Skype ID, Twitter @name, Facebook personal and business page URLs, etc.

Your educational experience: when, where, activities, and societies including higher education and continuing education (e.g. Dale Carnegie or Landmark Education, significant conference training, etc.).

Your contact information – Web URL, Phone Number, Street Address

Your educational experience: when, where, activities, and societies including higher education and continuing education (e.g. Dale Carnegie or Landmark Education, significant conference training, etc.).

## TIP

Have an unusual name or spelling like our good friend Gayl Murphy?

How can she increase her chances to be found when people know her name but not how to spell it?

Wouldn't it be great if people that mis-type your name could find you anyhow? LinkedIn already associates Mike and Michael, Pete and Peter are covered as well.

Gather up the possible mis-spellings and alternate spellings of your name in your word processing software. Put them in your Summary or at the bottom of a Job Description.

The Contact Settings section, a natural location for this, may not be searched by LinkedIn so avoid it.

Lori puts this in her profile as part of an early job description.

Common Spellings of my name: Lori, Laurie, Lorrie, Lorie, Laura, Lara (But it really is Lori!) and Ruff, Rough, Russ, Rugh, Ruph, Rolph (but again, it's really just Ruff... Lori Ruff, The LinkedIn Diva)!

# LinkedIn Profile Development Process

**There are different approaches to developing your profile: the most popular are the immersed (dive in) or the "chip away" approaches. The "RockTheWorld" book works well for either.**

Your LinkedIn Profile is a business biography about YOU. There are two methods for creating your masterpiece – Song by Song and Immersion.

The Immersion method may be what happens planned or not, as you find that you just can't put the book down. Yep, you're hooked. _"Don't stop"_ (Fleetwood Mac, 1977), keep on going.

It's the Double Album you get and listen to all the way through as soon as you get home from the record store. That is the effect RockTheWorld can have on you. We know because readers reach out with excitement to tell us so!

The Song-by-Song method involves chipping away at it, perhaps over a period of weeks or a month (probably no longer). This book's short chapters work very well with this approach.

It will be very important to use word processing software to write your profile. It lets you see the text, put in special formatting characters, back up your text and repurpose this text in other locations like Facebook.

Once you are signed up and have your provisions together there is one VERY IMPORTANT THING you must try:

Tune your radio to a classic rock (or your favorite) station and keep it kind of low. This sets the mood for the journey. It is amazing at how well this works and it is part of the whistle while we work principle, right?

The book is specifically segmented so that many of the sections can be completed in the time it takes to listen to a song. It's not by accident.

## Style 1 – Experience the full concert, the LP record

*Songwriting (LinkedIn Profile writing) done "Led Zeppelin style," like the Physical Graffiti double LP; Mike bought this album upon its release and still plays it today.*

If you start earlier in the day, this might just work for you. Have a pot of coffee or, better yet, a 6 pack of Mountain Dew, and some snacks. You may very well be like many others who get this book. They can't put it down. RockTheWorld was written in the wee hours and it is often experienced in the wee hours. Sorry if it is a bit addicting.

## Style 2 – Enjoy one song at a time, the 45 rpm record (Single)

*Songwriting (LinkedIn Profile writing) done "Beatles style,"*
*like a series of 45 rpm Singles*

Most chapters in this book should take a single song to complete as long as you have your provisions handy. In some sections, particularly Experience, here may be a lot of little things to do in repetition. Call it a bunch of early Beatles songs, each about 2 1⁄2 minutes long.

In some cases, like your Summary, you might need a really LONG song like *"Free Bird"* (Lynyrd Skynyrd, 1975) to get it all in. Heck, you may actually want to replay that one a few times – "and this bird will never change." Start editing (creating) your LinkedIn Profile right from the LinkedIn Home Page.

Look for the TAB labeled "Profile." From it you can select the "Edit Your Profile" or "View Your Profile" Menu Items. You will be using both options a lot.

# LinkedIn Profile Editing

**Your LinkedIn Profile is a process, one that has you looking more spiffin' all the time. See something catchy? Copy it, adapt it, make it your own!**

The more active you become on LinkedIn the more reference points you have to dress up your profile, to STAND OUT! Certain areas of your LinkedIn Profile matter more than others. Focus on the top, "above the fold" at first.

When Mike discovered that special symbols could be put in a LinkedIn Profile in 2008, he blogged on it and it's now a widespread best practice.

♦ *Dress right for the dance and you go to this dance and get invited to more*

## Your profile is weighted

The LinkedIn Profile is comprised of a number of sections and sub-sections and some are more important than others. Some are designed for people to see and others are more designed for computers and search engines.

LinkedIn and Google both have a relatively "Top Down" way of ordering search results. This affects how you show up in search results. Since we all want to be on Page 1, we will look into it here in the RockTheWorld book. This will all make lots of sense and it isn't hard.

## Editing and Formatting are limited

LinkedIn Profiles are rather bland compared to their counterparts at Google, Facebook, and the like. No bold, underline, italics, fonts, not even spelll checkkk.

There are no Previews in LinkedIn. Use your word processing software to write the text and SAVE it. Then COPY/PASTE it into your profile and Save on LinkedIn. There is no preview so you must save your edits to see them. Now, since you just may need to UNDO this sometime, you are covered – you used word processing software, right?

LinkedIn is pretty bland by most standards, but it is not without ANY formatting options. It just takes some knowhow to get it to "do some flips."

For starters, you can use ALL CAPS and any character available on your keyboard. For example! @ # $ % ^ & * ( ) - _ = + { } [ ] | \ " ' : ; ? / > . < , ~ `. You can still do a lot with upper case and lowercase letters, 10 digits, and these other standard keyboard characters. :

## TIP

LinkedIn allows a limited number of special characters to be inserted into LinkedIn Profiles. Look at the example LinkedIn Profile and our own to see what we mean and how those features might be used effectively in YOUR profile.

In Microsoft Word, these special characters can be found under "Symbols." Use the Word Help system to find out where they are in the menu structure. (DO NOT use outline formatting.

Here are some symbols that we recommend because they work well in LinkedIn:

Mike & Lori's favorite symbols │ ▌ ◊ ▶ ◀↔ ♦ • ♫)

**Editing your Profile**

LinkedIn makes it really easy to make edits to your Profile. You can do it from any page on LinkedIn. On the navigation bar, find the "Profile" TAB.

When you hold (or hover) your mouse over the word "Profile," a drop-down menu shows "Edit Profile," "View Profile," or "Recommendations."

Again, while making changes, we recommend you have two browser tabs open, one for Edit and one for View so you can easily toggle between the two views.

# Keyword Inventory

In its most fundamental element, there are two basic reasons people use LinkedIn: to find and to be found. When people are looking for a resource, product, service or individual, they most often use the "People Search" box at the top right of the navigation bar. Others will actually choose the LinkedIn Advanced Search screen. Because it is the easiest default action, searches by Keyword sorted by Relevance is the most popular type of search.

Other LinkedIn users that go to the Advanced People Search: select one of more of the following criteria, listed in decreasing order of importance:

- ♦ Keywords
- ♦ Name
- ♦ Job titles
- ♦ Companies

Knowing a little but about searching will aid in crafting your LinkedIn Profile. You might think that a little extra attention to keywords is probably a good thing, and you would be right. So, let's go over some strategies.

Take a look at things from the perspective of the user who might try to find someone like you. What words would they use to distill credible results from among the millions of LinkedIn users? Think in terms of their finding you for the purpose that you wish to be found.

Step one is to strategize and write down all the words and phrases you wish to be found under. What words describe what you have to offer? Using Long Tail Keywords, or rather multiple words or phrases that describe you is better.

It is easier to show up in the searches when you focus more on your niche than on the primary Headword, or single keyword for your profession. Take for example the headword "LinkedIn." You can imagine there is a lot of competition for that word. But just adding one additional keyword to create the phrase "LinkedIn Trainer" knocks out people focused on LinkedIn Consulting and other focus areas.

Of course, if you are focused on "Software Consulting" you may also want to include the phrase "Software Consultant" in your efforts to reach those who might be searching for one, the other, or maybe even both. Is this starting to make some sense?

Keyword variations help you be found! Try your old friend Thesaurus .com to get ideas here again . For example, you might list speak, speaker, speaking, train, trainer, training, author, writer.

Get the idea? You have keywords and variations of those keywords . If you only list "speaker" and someone searches on "speaking", the computer will not find you! Does this sound like Search Engine Optimization (SEO) for a Website?

You bet! Some good ways to find new words are to ask your newest customers how they found you. What were your new customers thinking of when they went looking for someone like you? You want to ask your new customers, because they haven't learned your language yet.

Ask them before they learn your glossary so you know how people who don't know you yet think of when they think of what you do!

If you have a Google AdWords account, what are the words that you use in it? Make sure those are in your profile. (If you work for a company and you don't know, ask your manager or marketing department for help here.)

What about your competitors? How are they found? What words or phrases are in their profile that fit you well? If they show up in search results, wouldn't you want to show up too? At least with them, if not ahead of them!

## TIP

Lori's favorite tool is Google Insights for Search. She checks the search popularity of related words and phrases so she knows which are more important to focus on.

# How Others See Your LinkedIn Profile

It comes down to what you look like from the outside and not on the "back end" so make sure you check the "audience view" of your LinkedIn Profile. "View" your profile from inside and outside of LinkedIn.

It is a best practice to craft your Profile section by section in a word processor, optimizing as you go. This "song by song" approach allows you to concentrate on the individual elements that eventually roll up into the perfect product: your LinkedIn Profile! It's like a great album, built and enjoyed one song at a time.

Periodically, it helps to see the big picture too, the complete layout. Look at _"The Man in the mirror"_ (Michael Jackson, 1988) and see how your entire LinkedIn Profile looks when it is all put together.

Print it out, walk around while reading it out loud so you really understand what you LOOK and SOUND like to others. Once you finish, copy and paste the elements online and view it as the rest of the world sees it.

You will find a handy pdf and printer icon in the blue box near the top of your profile to get a quick, formatted version of your LinkedIn Profile in your hands, either electronically or on paper.

Your profile isn't really about you; it's about others isn't it? It's about what they see of you, what they get to know about you, and what they think of you. It's about their perception of who you are and how you might help them.

As such, don't you think it might be a good idea to put yourself in the place of the viewer? Don't you check yourself in the mirror before you walk out the door?

*Looking at your LinkedIn Profile "as others see it"*

This View Profile option is particularly useful to see how your use of ALL CAPS, punctuation, and bullets looks to others. It is even more useful to check that every section that results in hotlinks (such as Interests, Groups and Associations, and School Activities). Look at it and adjust your profile where needed so you don't work so hard only to shoot a hole in your credibility on a technicality.

LinkedIn features a menu item, View Profile, on the Profile drop down menu for this exact purpose. You can see how others see you with all the word wrapping and formatting properly in place.

You should also type your LinkedIn Public Profile URL into an Internet browser address bar to see how your profile looks to people outside of LinkedIn and to check "Your Public Profile" settings. Remember that you can find your Public Profile URL as the last item in the Header section below Websites. We spoke about it in detail in the last section.

# LinkedIn Profile Components

When you break a LinkedIn Profile down into its pieces, it really doesn't seem so hard to get to the finish line. Think of it as a concert or a movie, layered into songs and scenes.

It might seem a bit cold here, but YOU are essentially a record in a database called LinkedIn. It is like a spreadsheet behind the scenes and a Web site in front of the user.

*"I feel like a number"* (Bob Seger, 1981) is what you should feel like when you think of how many users are on LinkedIn today. Mike is LinkedIn user #125,841, Lori is #3,173,651. This is our LinkedIn ID #. To see what YOUR LinkedIn number is, look to the URL bar at the top when viewing your profile.

## Your LinkedIn Profile components

Notice the major LinkedIn Profile sections, in their default order of appearance and how they resemble songs on a record or on a CD. Is it a coincidence?

In this book, you will find great ideas on what to include, where to include them and how to optimize your profile to be found in searches. Everything has a home and some things have multiple homes, enhancing your find-ability.

- ◆ Name
- ◆ Headline
- ◆ Geographic Area (where you live)
- ◆ Industry (that you work in)
- ◆ Summary (text about you)
- ◆ Specialties (keywords about you)
- ◆ Experience (company, job title, period, description)
- ◆ Education (schooling & professional training)
- ◆ Additional Information (Websites, Twitter IDs, Interests, Groups and Associations, Personal Information)
- ◆ LinkedIn Groups
- ◆ Contact Settings
- ◆ Additional Sections can be added to your profile and placed where you want them... more on that later

# Chapter Three

## "Above The Fold"

The analogies between your LinkedIn profile and a newspaper are many and it is most evident here. Some areas are very basic (name, location, industry) then it interesting with your professional headline (like a newspaper headline), your headshot photo and the external links you include in your profile.

## Basics

The Basic Profile shows only your Name, Industry, Location and the Number of Recommendations you have.

## Additional Options

- Photo
- Headline
- Summary with or without Specialties
- Current Positions with or without details
- Past Positions with or without details
- Educations with or without details
- Websites
- Interests
- Groups and Associations
- Honors and Awards
- Interested in... (the 8 check boxes you select with your Contact Settings... why people should contact you)

As you add Additional Sections to your profile, you'll be able to select those as well. For example, Volunteer Experiences & Causes, Projects, Languages, Publications, Certifications, Skills, Courses, and the new Honors and Awards.

The illustration above shows you what the Public Profile screen looks like and how the check boxes work.

Once again, we highly recommend you include all of the items available, unless you have a good reason not to. The question you should ask for each option is "Why Not?" versus "Why?"

The LinkedIn Header is a collection (and display) of the most important parts of your LinkedIn Profile. The very location, right at the top of the profile, is a clue as to its importance. Marketers call it "above the fold" and music fans call it a "Greatest Hits."

The LinkedIn Header is a bit like your 30-second elevator pitch. Even with the Header, there are areas that are more important than others. *"Welcome to the machine"* (Pink Floyd, 1975).

Here are the "contents" of the LinkedIn Profile Header.

**Picture** – Use it to build trust

**Headline** – your tagline; the most important 120 characters in your profile

**Status** – updates that others see in their Network Update stream

**Location** – e.g. Greater Minneapolis-St. Paul Area

**Industry** – selected from LinkedIn's rather limited list

**Current Position(s)** * – the top 3 current positions with links to the Company Page when it exists

**Past Positions** * – up to 3, with links to the Company Page when it exists

**Education** * – up to 3 of the most recent entries

**Recommendations** – The number is how many you choose to display, not the entire sum, Mike has over 300 Recommendations yet only shows 100 of the best.

**Connections** * - # of direct connections up to 500+ with a link to display them

**Websites** * – up to 3 can be entered (with custom link labels no less)

**Twitter address** – link one or several Twitter accounts to your profile

**Profile URL** * - The "www." address for your LinkedIn Profile

*\* Denotes information that is summarized from other areas of the profile.*

As you can see, your Header is more of a collection of information than content. People, as well as search bots will view this from top down as they scroll through your profile. In the coming pages, we will go through each of these areas in greater detail. Don't worry, it will be plenty fun.

# What's in a Name?

**If you do funny things with your name, people may not be able to find you, while others may discount you as unprofessional and select someone else. Worse yet, including anything in your name field other than your name or lettered credentials can get you booted off LinkedIn!**

Prince, Madonna and Pink can get by with one word names, BUT YOU CAN'T. You see a lot of fancy things happening with names and most are NOT things you want to emulate.

While your NAME seems really simple, there are some rather significant strategies to consider. Women have the biggest issues because of marriage. Lettered credentials are OK in this field. email addresses, monikers, business names, and numbers of connections are not OK!

There are some of the "cute" things people do in order to standout, to get people to invite them. In the LinkedIn space what gets you ahead in one area, gets you behind in another. So, be really SIMPLE with your name. For most, the best technique is FirstName LastName.

**First Name**

Your First Name is just that. Use what someone calls you in conversation. They call me "Mike" so my name says Mike.

Certain professions are more formal and that needs to be taken into account. In that case, Mike may be listed as Michael. Use the name you use when you introduce yourself at a networking event. If you introduce yourself to strangers with your formal name rather than your nickname, use that here as well.

LinkedIn does a good job showing search results that include common nicknames (i.e., Bob Plant and Robert Plant are considered the same, same thing for James Page, Jim Page and Jimmy Page).

Hey Junior!

There are obvious examples where Jr. and Sr. (or Junior) apply. Do what looks/ feels right. If you are commonly known by this name and someone is going to search for you this way than do it this way.

If you're a "Jr." and no one knows, don't include it here either. We have had an instance where a father and son were both on LinkedIn and we agree, at first it seemed confusing... until we realized they were both in very different professions and most people looking for someone by name will likely have an idea of what profession the person they are looking for is in.

## Last Name

Your Last name should also be obvious with a few exceptions. Don't put in anything but your current Last Name with the exception of lettered credentials that are common in SOME industries.

Some examples include PMP, CPA, PhD, MD, J.D or Esq. There are very FEW lettered credentials that qualify and LION is NOT one of them. So, use them with great care. If it doesn't look very professional, think again about using it. Do not use the full name of your credentials, letters only.

## Middle or Former Name

Use this field if it applies and then only with careful consideration and if you need to identify yourself to former contacts. Again, the case is for find-ability. Who knows you by the former name; how long ago did you use it? If it was recent, do it. If not, don't.

Think about privacy issues. Will you be making it easier for someone to threaten the integrity of your identity if you disclose your maiden name freely? As user privacy advocates, Lori and I recognize it is a matter of public record, but how easy do you want to make it?

If your children are young it is likely as much of an issue for you as this might be for those of us with children who are working adults.

Again though, if using the Middle or Former Name field will help people identify that they have the right "you", go ahead and use it!

# TIP

Have an unusual name or spelling like our friend Gayl Murphy? Notice she doesn't spell her name Gayle with an "e". Another spelling might be Gail.

How can she increase her chances of being found when people know her name but not how to spell it?

Wouldn't it be great if people could misspell your name and find you anyhow? LinkedIn already associates Mike and Michael. It offers some help for Tom, Art and Rob as well.

So, here's the trick – gather up the possible mis-spellings and alternate spellings of your name and put them in an area of your profile. If there is room in the Summary, fine, otherwise, try an area like the bottom of a Job Description.

We suggest the bottom of a job description or another place you are comfortable with. The LinkedIn Contact Settings section, a great natural place, may not be searched by LinkedIn so this is not a good place.

Lori puts this in her profile as part of an early job description

Common Spellings of my name: Lori, Laurie, Lorrie, Lorie, Laura, Lara (But it really is Lori!) and Ruff, Rough, Russ, Rugh, Ruph, Rolph (but again, it's really just Ruff... Lori Ruff, The LinkedIn Diva)!

# Ground Zero, Your LinkedIn Location

**LinkedIn uses Zip Codes and not the actual name of your city to determine YOUR OFFICIAL "LOCATION".**

LinkedIn's "Location Field" is probably one of the easiest things to complete. Supply a Zip Code and LinkedIn matches you up with your metropolitan areas. Understanding how LinkedIn works behind the scenes will help you get more precise in your searches and in your listings.

Everyone has a hometown, especially on LinkedIn. When you first sign up for LinkedIn you are prompted for a Zip Code rather than a city. That's a clue.

There are always issues with Zip Codes and cities. *"My Hometown"* (Bruce Springsteen, 1989) couldn't be from New Jersey, for example. New Jersey's biggest star ever maps back to the Greater New York City Area or the Greater Philadelphia Area.

Many locations are (or were) rolled up into "Greater" areas – Greater Denver Area, Greater San Francisco Area, Greater Minneapolis-St. Paul Area.

Upon entering your Zip Code you now have options. Do I want to be specifically from "my city" or do I want to be part of something bigger. This screen shot illustrates the point.

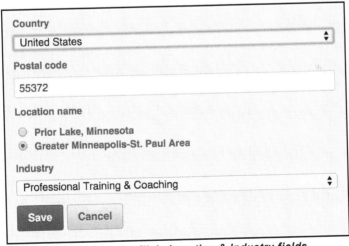

*The LinkedIn Profile's Location & Industry fields*

The jury is out, but we are sticking with the Greater areas for searching reasons. People don't look for Prior Lake or Savage or Bloomington as much as they do Minneapolis, even though people may live in one town and work in another.

For example, people often include a Zip Code in advanced searches. Will it more often be for Minneapolis or Prior Lake, which is 45 miles away? It depends on the radius of the search. It can be as little as 10 miles radius from the edge of the zip code, or 100. The default is 50.

No hometown? If you NEED to, you can leave the Zip Code field blank and you will ultimately be listed as United States or your country rather than the region.

Many current LinkedIn users should revisit this area, as there are new options for your Location, or your hometown. Change it if you need to.

It's easy to change or edit this information. From the Profile TAB, select "Edit Profile," then click the "edit" link beside your name. You can also access the "Name and Location" edit screen from the LinkedIn Settings Screen (Under the Profile tab and "Helpful Links").

# Your Industry according to LinkedIn

**The real question is whether your industry is YOUR industry or your company's industry and the jury is out.**

Your "Industry" can be a marketing issue for some and a corporate policy issue for others. Here's the skinny…

The "Industry" is important as it shows in your Header and in your Digital Footprint. You only get to pick ONE and you can change it all you like. You must choose from LinkedIn's list and many people feel their industry is NOT on the list.

### Industry Strategy

QUICK ANSWER - Pick something from the list and get on with it. If you do SEO work (and they don't list SEO as an option), pick something related, like Internet. Just don't pick something inaccurate.

A LITTLE MORE THOUGHT - A little strategizing will help. Look around and see what others are doing in your company, in your industry, in your "circles." Corporate policies also help you decide what to put in for your LinkedIn Industry.

In searches, one can limit search results by industry or industries so give it some strategic thought.

Teams have issues and the answer is standardization. Managers should pick one industry, perhaps with help from the marketing department.

Remember, you can easily change your mind later and with a quick "Edit" of your profile, make that change happen.

# LinkedIn Profile Headline – Your Elevator Pitch

**Like the Headline of a newspaper, the LinkedIn Headline is an advertisement for the rest of the story, for the whole paper (LinkedIn Profile); limited space limits the fluff.**

Your headline is a series of words or phrases that are there to attract the search engines as well to be catchy to the human eye.

Your Headline is what accompanies your name on the marquis. It is a short elevator speech on display in the LinkedIn world. It is the MOST IMPORTANT PART OF YOUR ENTIRE LINKEDIN PROFILE. Focus major attention here!!!

Your message must LEAP OFF THE PAGE. You ideally want your Headline to _"Shout it Out Loud"_ (KISS, 1977).

In short, include attractive/important keywords and short phrases and then arrange them like artwork. Include words that describe you, your service, perhaps your client base and make them look really nice!

If the song doesn't catch you in the first few chords, you might just switch channels. The same is true for LinkedIn and how you look in search results.

The Headline represents you to the professional networking world of LinkedIn. It's the highlight of your Digital Footprint on LinkedIn and it's what appears when someone searches for you with Google. A good headline attracts people to click on your profile from a list of others. Then your Summary converts them to interested parties.

The Headline is brief, only 120 characters max. No carriage returns are allowed at all and only single spaces are allowed so formatting it to look really nice is a bit of an art.

Use at least 110 of your 120 characters!

**LinkedIn is surprisingly helpful...**

For example, if you type too many characters in most profile fields, it will reject the change and indicate 1) how many characters you are allowed; and 2) tell you how many you have used. You do have to do the math however. It's a nifty feature that saves guessing.

**Here are some examples of short headlines (less effective):**

"President, Strategic Systems LLC"
"Business Coach"
"Sr. Sales Manager, MCI"
"Executive Recruiter specializing in IT"

**Now here are some more advanced headlines. Notice the difference:**

"CEO, CommonCraft Ventures LLC, investing in green energy concerns"

"Sr. Development Manager, INFO for The Go, developers of mobile applications for the Oil and Gas Industry"

"Chief Operating Officer (COO), Managed Hosting PLC, managed data center solutions for streaming media"

**Here are some excellent headlines from real people on LinkedIn:**

"▶ When you need Managed Services, Think IT!◀ Fully Managed IT Consulting serving Public, Private, Business& Education"

"Regional VP, MegaStar Financial ♦ Founder, Holst Mortgage ♦ Residential Finance Expert"

"Host of the Most Positive Business Radio Show | Customer Service Expert | Best Selling Author | 2011 Influential Leader"

"CEO, Integrated Alliances ♦ Corporate B2B LinkedIn Sales Trainer ♦ Keynote Speaker, Social Media Futurist, ENFP"

### Headlines and Teams

Are you on a team? How do you personalize the Headline it doesn't look like another teammate's? Let's look at what our client, PrideStaff does:

"PrideStaff | PrideStaff Financial | An owner-operated firm providing client experiences based on what they value most"

"SVP, Field Operations | National Staffing and Recruiting Firm | Staff Development | Passionate Client Service"

"EVP/COO, Vendor Management, Risk Management, Staff Development | PrideStaff: National Recruiting & Staffing Organization"

And another team for Catalyst Resources:

> UI – User Interface Design & Development | Managing Partner –Lead Solution Architect | Critical SaaS Solutions Delivered

> UI – User Interface Design & Development I Contract Staffing I Account & Project Management

**It's all relative**

Your LinkedIn profile headline is a process and not a project. Visit it often and mix it up a bit. Some pointers:

1. Look at other people's headlines to see what you like and what looks good for you.
2. Look in similar occupations to see what they are doing. Ask them if their headline has been effective (why copy someone who looks good but isn't getting Profile Views?)
3. Check around with friends (those on LinkedIn) who know you professionally and ask what they think.

Seek to be MUCH BETTER than the others. After all, you have RockTheWorld powers now! Realize, of course, that others too have read this book and have these powers as well.

**TIP**

**Word is the Word}**

So, using your Word processor, create severalHeadline variations one after the other and see how they look relative to one another. Save the file then, after spell checking, pick the best one and copy and paste it into the Headline Field (You will need to be in Edit Profile mode). Return to this file later and rotate in a different headline.

# Whenever I see your smiling face ...

**Having no photo ensures that people won't click or connect and most will never come back.**

A photo in LinkedIn is an absolute MUST. People will not take you seriously without one. People choose to do business with people they can have a relationship with and that means SEEING YOU. It is suspicious and, for some, disrespectful to hide behind an icon on ANY Social Media site.

Do you look at the record cover, the CD cover, the DVD cover? Of course you do. We're more visual than ever in this YouTube world. Don't make the mistake of being any more anonymous than you have to on LinkedIn.

No photo makes others think 1) you forgot, 2) you couldn't figure out how to do it, or 3) you didn't think it was important. None of these are good reasons.

So, include a good photo. It's easy. An iPhone does one dandy job.If you have an iPhone or Android phone you can use the LinkedIn application to take your photo and put it directly on your LinkedIn profile. It works great.

Your picture is the heart of your Digital Footprint, making it so very important to your success on LinkedIn. It really "sets the tone" for the reader of your profile.

## Credibility and Trust in a Virtual World

Your photo must portray you as credible, approachable and real. It should be professional and reflect your status or profession. For example,a friend of ours is a photographer. He has a headshot of himself holding his camera. You can still see his eyes, but it is clear from his photo that he is serious about his work.

When you upload your photo, crop it as close to your face as you can. It needs to show a real person who is approachable and willing to help.

Here are some good LinkedIn photo examples with a sense of personal style.

It's a photo of you and just you – a headshot for most, although creative types can "explore the space" a bit. The LinkedIn license agreement says:

A photo is worth 1,000 words or $10,000. Have your profile photo touched up by a pro and see how it boosts your success on LinkedIn. A little Photoshop to lighten it, remove a "spot", remove some wild hairs. For most, we suggest a pure white background. This is best with a transparent image and that means a PNG file (vs. a JPG).

Def Leppard _("Photograph"_, 1983), Paul Simon and Kid Rock/Sheryl Crow all made money from "photos" and so can you! Invest a little in it and get a lot out.

While your LinkedIn thumbnail picture is small, just 80 pixels by 80 pixels, it can be clicked on and expanded to 450 pixels by 450 pixels. Still, at this size, even a basic camera phone photo will suffice from a resolution standpoint.

Don't have a graphics person who can do this for you? Check out _www.GraphicBreeze.com_ for some expert help.

## Joel Comm

*www.linkedin.com/in/joelcomm*

Author, Speaker, Entrepreneur, Consultant | NY Times Best Seller | "Twitter Power" | Motivating & Inspiring Worldwide

## Jeffrey Gitomer

*www.linkedin.com/in/jeffreygitomer*

Best-Selling Author | Professional Speaker | Sales Expert

## Ron Noden

*www.linkedin.com/in/ronnoden*

Chief Development Officer at LifeScale Analytics

## Terry Sullivan

*www.linkedin.com/in/terrysullivanmba*

Marketing Director | Strategy, Execution & Results | Success with Creativity & Vision... Ready for Hire!

## Paul Giurata

*www.linkedin.com/in/giurata*

*UI – User Interface Design & Development | Managing Partner/ Lead Solution Architect | Critical SaaS Solutions Delivered*

On a team? You can solve a lot of headaches for folks by having a photographer show up at the office or company event, conference, etc. to take pictures of the team. PrideStaff, a client of ours, did precisely this at their annual conference. Be sure that the photos make your team look approachable rather than the typical stuffy website portraits many companies use.

**The team pictures for PrideStaff.**

| | |
|---|---|
|  | *Tammi Heaton*<br><br>COO/EVP, Vendor & Risk Management, Staff Development \| National Recruiting & Franchise Staffing Organization |
|  | *John-Reed McDonald*<br><br>SVP, Field Operations \| National Staffing and Recruiting Firm \| Staff Development \| Passionate Client Service |
|  | *Michael Eckelman*<br><br>PrideStaff \| PrideStaff Financial \| An owner-operated firm providing client experiences based on what they value most |

To upload your photo:

1. You must first click on "Edit Profile" to get into edit mode.
2. Then, click on "Edit Your Photo" in the header area.
3. Select "Choose File," browse to the photo you want to import. It needs to be less than 4 MB.
4. Click "Upload Photo" and use the LinkedIn photo-cropping tool to zoom in on your smilin' face.
5. Choose who can see your photo ... My Connections; My Network; or Everyone. We recommend selecting "Everyone."
6. Click "Save Settings."

# Driving Web Site Traffic With LinkedIn

**Your LinkedIn Profile can direct click traffic to a number of other really useful places, so use all 3 links to generate business traffic!**

Putting Websites on your LinkedIn Profile is a no-brainer – simple and powerful. After all, driving traffic to your Web site is a science, the subject matter of volumes of books and tons of experts. You might even include THIS book in that category. After all, social media has opened up a whole new area of expertise for SEO experts.

LinkedIn lets you include three links on your LinkedIn Profile in an area called Websites. It is really a place to list anything with a URL that you want someone to click on and visit.

### What to Link To

Don't waste any of your 3 links on Twitter or on blogs. LinkedIn has better ways to handle those properties.

Some other ideas:

- Facebook Page (or a profile if you don't have a page)
- Google+ profile
- YouTube video or channel
- PDF File
- Landing page for a target audience
- Company job listings
- Creative portfolio
- Join a mailing list

### Truth in Link Listing

Let's talk about trust again. Don't you like to know where a link will take you before you click?

A LinkedIn website text link like 'My Company" doesn't inspire people to click as much as something like "RockTheWorld Website." LinkedIn can drive traffic to your selected sites by letting you enter customized link text to encourage clicks.

*"Two out of three ain't bad"* (Meatloaf, 1977) but three out of three is better. LinkedIn gives you room for up to 3 Websites and we suggest you use them all.

Here's an instance of "more is better." Why stop with one link, one Web site? Get two or three, even if they just point to different pages on the same website. Got a YouTube Channel, Facebook Page, something else with a URL to share?

If you work for a company that has a website, by all means use it. If you have your own business website, use it. Personal websites require a bit of self-restraint. Consider them only where they are relevant to your purpose for being on LinkedIn.

By all means consider website sub-pages you may wish to direct people to (a jobs board, a "Contact Us" page, etc.). This is a very good place for that activity.

Here are your options from the LinkedIn drop down list:

- ♦ My Website
- ♦ My Company
- ♦ My Blog
- ♦ My RSS Feed
- ♦ My Portfolio
- ♦ Other

Some options are better than others and "Other" is the CLEAR WINNER.

The "Other" option lets you key in a Custom Text Label and you want to do this in all cases. Suggestions might include "RockTheWorld Web Site," "My Company on Facebook," "Learn more about me," "See examples of my Work" or even "Search our Jobs."

*Replace the default LinkedIn Profile Web Link text with a custom label*

You can actually make money with this technique as well. For example, if you are a member of an affiliate program, where you make money if people click on a link and buy something, you can use this to direct people to the site. But use care - keep it relevant and professional.

For example, if you are an affiliate for a Webinar program, you could insert a text label like, "Find Business Webinars Here" and then enter the URL, probably something like _www.WebinarsForThoseWhoRock.com/?AF=2121_ and it will handle the behind the scenes work like you would expect.

Some examples of our URL's of interest to others:

- ◆ Company Web Site
- ◆ Company Jobs Page
- ◆ Facebook Company Page
- ◆ Get Our Newsletter
- ◆ View Our YouTube Channel

## When 3 URL's isn't enough

There are some workarounds for those of us that just can't live with just 3 URL's. For example, we each have between 15 and 20 active Social Media URL's.

So, what's a LinkedIn user to do with room for just 3 URL's?

There are some options, really good options actually. One such option is ItsMyURL's(_www.ItsMyURLs.com_). This site consolidates your URL's and adds some nifty features of its own.

Mike uses a Text Label on his LinkedIn Profile named "See ALL my Networks & Links." ItsMyURLs is his 3rd link. It takes clickers to a site that consolidates his Social Media links and Web sites. It also includes a nifty background picture, special friends, a short BIO, even a custom "QR code."

The URLs we use here are _www.MikeIsOnline.com_, _www.LoriIsOnline.com_ and _www.RockstarNetworking.com._ and they all redirect people to our ItsMyURLs pages.

# You Are Your LinkedIn URL

**Turn on your whole LinkedIn Profile for viewing by visitors inside LinkedIn and outside. (WYSIWIG = What You See Is What You Get)**

There is a lot of chatter about Privacy in the social platforms. LinkedIn makes privacy control easy so you can dictate what information others can see about you (particularly for your profile section visibility and member feed). For the most part, you want to be as open, visible, and available as possible. After all, you are here to be found.

Don't fret too much over hiding public information. Why tell the story then shut it off so people can't hear how brilliant you are? Lori speaks at conferences internationally about Social Networking Privacy, talking to security professionals about the concerns that Users voice to us. We understand your concerns and we work to educate you about prudent use, particularly on LinkedIn. Frankly, LinkedIn makes it easy. You just have to know what options are available for you and how to adjust them.

One particularly nifty related LinkedIn feature is giving your LinkedIn Profile a custom URL (you know that www. thing that gets people to you). Create an easy to remember name that is a bit more "friendly." You can use this nice looking URL on business cards, in email signatures, and more!

_www.linkedin.com/in/mikeoneil_ or _www.linkedin.com/in/loriruff_

Want success from LinkedIn? Take Steppehwolf's '67 advice: "Get your motor running, head out on the highway, looking for adventure in whatever comes our way." When deciding which sections of your LinkedIn Profile to make public (to the public outside of LinkedIn) check all the boxes. You can reel it in again if there is something you decide you don't want to share with the outside world.

But again, the point of being on LinkedIn, of doing all this work, is to be found. Un-checking boxes here only means the information is not available to people who are not logged into LinkedIn.

When bands head to the studio to cut a record, they use lots of mixing equipment to get it just right. Everything is cut in raw form, then refined, mixed, and released._"See me, feel me"_ (The Who, 1970) might be more like See (just the right amount of) Me, Feel (just the right amount of) Me, as you select what you wish to show and what you choose to hide from the world outside of LinkedIn.

When you turn "off" a section, it does not affect the search or views inside of LinkedIn; it is just hidden from viewers outside of LinkedIn. In order for them to see it, the viewer will have to log into LinkedIn or create an account.

In general, you want people searching on LinkedIn AND those searching out on the Internet so find you. That's why you are on LinkedIn, isn't it?

Remember, people finding your LinkedIn Profile through Internet searches cannot see all of your profile (e.g. your Contact Settings or Personal Information) until they log into LinkedIn. Some information (such as Personal Information) is only visible to your Tier 1 connections.

Note that this is also an area where you can get the cool LinkedIn Profile Badge to promote your profile on your website, email signature, etc. Once you click through to the options page, there are lots of choices, but for the most part, it looks something like this:

*The LinkedIn Profile Badge for Web sites and blogs*

You get to the Public Profile area through Edit Profile, then look down at the BOTTOM of your Header. It should look something like this:

*Getting to your LinkedIn Public Profile Page*

Once you click Edit, the Public Profile options that LinkedIn gives are extensive. Don't worry, it's easy actually. Just click all the boxes, TURN EVERYTHING ON

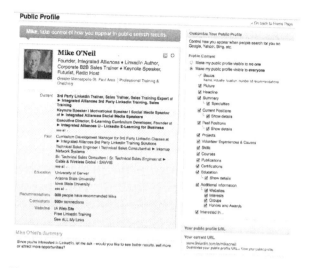

*Your LinkedIn Public Profile Page (Mike in this case)*

## No One

This will hide your profile from everyone doing a web search. It is as if you (or at least your LinkedIn Profile does not exist. However, when people log into LinkedIn, they can still find your profile.

If you have your name set to first name, last initial, and your Public Profile set to "None," people within LinkedIn but outside of your network will see "PRIVATE" in place of your name.

## Everyone

When you let Everyone see your profile, you create the maximum benefit and open the most doors for yourself. LinkedIn is an open environment and that's the value in it. We recommend you select "Everyone".

# Chapter Four

## In Summary...

Tell your story just "below the fold" in one single section. It's your summary and it's a bit like a cover letter that accompanies a resume or a bio that is read about a speaker just before they take the stage. Your LinkedIn profile summary "sums it all up" and we focus on that and that alone in this chapter.

The Summary Section of your LinkedIn Profile is about the future, it is about tomorrow, it's not about *"Living in the past"* (Jethro Tull, 1972) although we really do enjoy their music. "Aqualung" anyone?

For the most part, the Summary is a conversation you have with your reader. If you compare it to introducing yourself at a professional networking event, a conversation that crosses into personal, you are not far off base.

So, what is your value statement? What things from your past have relevance going forward NOW? Which experiences qualify you to do business brilliantly today? What makes you interesting? These are the items to focus your Summary text attention on.

Your LinkedIn profile summary is FROM you more than it is ABOUT you. That means it is NOT written in the third person. People should feel as if they just met you when they finish reading your summary.

The Summary should state in concise terminology what you can do for others going forward, what you bring to the table. It's the 80/20 rule, 80 percent what you can do for others, 20 percent what you seek from others (how readers can help you).

In keeping with our musical journey through the LinkedIn Profile, the Summary is more than "just another song". It's more like a rock medley. Think *"Suite Judy Blue Eyes"* from Crosby Still Nash & Young (1976), a series of songs melded together that paint a picture.

After your Professional Headline, your Summary is the perhaps single most important part of your LinkedIn profile. Spend considerable time and attention here. DO NOT simply paste in your resume. A resume typically looks 90 percent backward and ten percent forward. Your LinkedIn Profile is the opposite. It is almost all forward-looking!

If your Headline is the attention grabber that draws people to your profile, your Summary is where you get to tell the "rest of the story", where you let people know whether the meant to find you or not, now that they are here, you are worth knowing! "Back it up". This is where you establish your credibility once they land on your profile.

## From vs. About

The profile is a dialogue FROM you to the reader. It is NOT a biography ABOUT YOU. It is NOT to be written in the 3rd person. Let's take a look at the opening statement of Ed Redwood's Summary:

An IT and telecommunications specialist, I run a team of consultants and partners that help over 500 small- and medium-sized businesses across the UK achieve their goals through the use of technology.

That's much more of an introduction than what this same information might look and sound like in the third person:

Mr. Redwood is an IT and telecommunications specialist. He runs a team of consultants and partners that help over 500 small- and medium-sized businesses across the UK achieve their goals through the use of technology.

In the second example, you just read about someone, in the first, he actually introduced himself to you! When you read a Summary FROM him rather than ABOUT him, you get the feeling you've just had a conversation with him.

Use this space to duplicate how you introduce yourself to a perfect potential customer or business partner, like at a networking event. What do you typically say, better yet, what would you like to say? What questions to people ask you and how do you answer?

With the Summary, you have about 2/3 of a printed page (2,000 characters) and you will want to occupy all of this space when you are all set and done.

Remember, if you go over the 2,000, LinkedIn will tell you how many characters you have entered and how many you have left when you cut and paste your profile text here. That's a really nifty feature.

Within the Summary section itself, the first few paragraphs are the most important just like a newspaper article or any other published text.

IN NO CASE should you use LinkedIn's Import Resume Feature. This will create a whole lot of needless editing. Use the principles in this book instead.

# The Summary Game Plan

This section requires its own game plan. The first sentence or two of your LinkedIn Summary should be very clear about what you do. It is your value statement. It will tell people why they should keep reading... or not.

For sales professionals it may include the types of companies you work with, what solutions you offer and what makes you special. It is a 20 second elevator pitch. You will get a chance to embellish it in the coming paragraphs.

Spread it out. Keep paragraphs to no more than 5 lines (not sentences) total. If they get bigger, just cut them in half. Use "white space" to keep it readable.

Here's an example for our client PrideStaff's SVP _John-Reed McDonald_. It's short for a LinkedIn Summary, but it's powerful.

What does it mean for me to be the Sr. Vice President of the Premier National Recruiting Organization mean? For me, it means being able to live my passion with high energy.

The reason I chose PrideStaff is that they mirror my own values and mission: to affect the business and personal lives of my friends in a positive way.

I maintain focus on company goals by helping senior management train and mentor their teams to provide exceptional service focused on what their clients value most.

In every engagement, we encourage our team to interact in a way that makes the client relationship personal and builds loyalty. We treat candidates with respect and as unique individuals throughout the employment process. We bring both sides together in a meaningful way that provides a win/win/win for all.

Are you ready to change your life? Call (559-449-5831) or email me (jmcdonald@pridestaff.com) today.

Notice how he builds a desire within the reader that is his target audience to want to do business with him and PrideStaff? *And notice to how he ends with a powerful call to action.*

## Fancy it up

Use special formatting characters to make it interesting and to serve as bullets to help draw the reader's eye down the page. But don't overdo it! You may have used some of these special characters in your Headline already. If so, you may choose to use the same characters or to use complimentary ones that support your message.

Use the first 1/4 of your summary to GET PEOPLE INTERESTED IN YOU. You are not appealing to everybody, but rather to your target audience. This is who you're writing for. Use language that will ATTRACT them.

Write several short paragraphs about who you are and what you have to offer; what value do you bring the reader?

It is okay if what you write might turn some people away. They are self-opting out and they will do so without interrupting your day with questions that will probably result in a "no sale" anyway!

The next part of your summary should be about your company, your employer.

**Work for a mid-to-large sized company? Try this:**

 ♦ What does the company do?
 ♦ Who are your customers (types)?
 ♦ What makes the company and their products/services special?
 ♦ Where do you fit into the larger picture? Location and department, perhaps?

**Work for a small company (not self-employed)? Make it a little less about the organization.**

- ♦ What does the company do?
- ♦ Who are your customers (types)?
- ♦ What makes the company and their products/services special?
- ♦ How do I contribute to the success of the company?

**Self-employed or work for yourself? It becomes more about you.**

- ♦ Your role as the "chief" and what makes you special?
- ♦ What inspired you to start the business?
- ♦ What does your product or service do?
- ♦ How did you get to this point?
- ♦ What in your past lends credibility to what you do now?

Next, give people a wrap-up of your background as it pertains to today and to the future. What have you done that matters NOW?

If you have done things that are relevant going forward—experiences, projects, contacts—this is good to include next (the last third or so of the Summary. The key here is what you are doing NOW and that it is relevant.

You might then wrap up with what inspires you, what you like to do when you are not in the center of your business universe. It is nice to finish with something personal and a call to action. Keep it simple and concise just like John-Reed's above or here's how Lori ends her Summary:

We are authentic & want to help YOU achieve YOUR goals. Call 303-683-9600 today or email my team: training@integratedalliances.com.

Use action words and not typical descriptive text. Remember, there are over 100 Million people on LinkedIn and you need to stand out in this important crowd.

What's it really look like? You saw how it started, so let's look at the full summary of our client and friend _Ed Redwood_ to give you the full picture of another great Summary (notice how he uses bullets to help make key points stand out, draw the eye down the page, and:

An IT and telecommunications specialist, I run a team of consultants and partners that help over 500 small and medium-sized businesses across the UK achieve their goals through the use of technology.

When clients hire Think IT, they hire one of five principal team members whose expertise enables them to manage and monitor all delivery of services. We match our clients to the right specialist to match their unique culture and needs. I've had great success hiring and training a team of professionals better than myself.

**Our client benefits include:**

### Increased productivity

- Shorter recovery period in disaster recovery
- Disaster recovery planning
- Reduced down time
- Completely Integrated Services
- One Bill to cover CCTV, Communications, IT & Hosting
- Your Own IT Technology Department

### Increased profits

- Lower total cost of ownership of computer technology
- Lower cost in ongoing call costs of client phone systems
- Managed Ongoing Services Fixed Monthly Fee

### Increased flexibility

- More manageable assets
- Flexible Finance
- Flexible support terms
- Contracts or On Demand Services
- Choice of In House, Hosted or Hybrid Cloud Solutions

It's been nearly 20 years since I started my own IT consulting firm. Having previously worked in corporate technology sales for 3 companies in 5 years, I tuned a skill for troubleshooting and management into an opportunity to help SMBs tap into the best in technology for their business.

Rather than corporate sales, I took a decidedly different track in managed IT consulting, where my success was tied to that of my clients rather than to the next big sale. In my first 5 years, I built a solid client base that has sustained my success ever since.

If you need someone you can trust to manage your IT infrastructure, I'm your man.

▶ **Call me or my team at 01582 817000 or email sales@thinkits.com** ◀

## Thesaurus

For example - are you "experienced" or are you a "seasoned veteran" or an "industry expert?" You get the idea. We encourage you to think like a super thesaurus for just this purpose. There are other variants of a printed Thesaurus, such as www.m-w.com, and they are very good as well.

*The Thesaurus.com Web site, a favorite tool of The LinkedIn Rockstars*

Two great sources for ideas on words is www.Thesaurus.com. the book "Words That Sell." BOTH were used in the writing of this book.

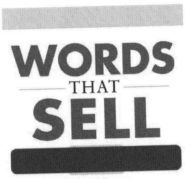

*The "Words That Sell" book by Richard Bayan,*
*another favorite tool of The LinkedIn Rockstars*

### It's hard to stand out

**Let me use an analogy to illustrate why words can be so important.**

- When you were in high school, maybe you were near the top of your class. Then you went to college and there were others there who were the top of their class, making you average. The same analogy works for sports, from high school to college to the pros, the competition gets tougher as the pool of people who continue in the expertise gets smaller.
- Now you're on LinkedIn and that definitely sets you apart. You have an edge over all those people that are NOT on LinkedIn. On the flip side, you are now part of millions of LinkedIn users. The analogy above has meaning here as well. Among those millions of users, there is a subset within your area of expertise. How do you rank; how do you stand up to your competition?

Why do we bring this up? Well, this is a pep talk aimed at inspiring you to make your LinkedIn Profile special; or even better, a bit "sexy." You will look at profiles through a different eye now. Be on the lookout for things that "catch your eye". Maybe you can use ideas that look good on other profiles, or a variation of them in your own.

You want to be the _"Shining Star"_ (Earth Wind and Fire, 1978) the one that stands out. The Summary, as well as the Headline, is where to STAND OUT. These two fields more than any other will be the reason people decide you're the one to call. Make sure they can reach you!

**Keep on the Lookout**

Look at our profiles and those of our highlighted case studies for some really advanced Summary and Headline ideas. Be warned: you may not be ready or able to do all of these things. Consider them perpetual prototypes. Keep in mind that we've been working on our profiles for years and continue to constantly monitor and massage them.

Mike's LinkedIn Profile:: _www.linkedin.com/in/mikeoneil_

Lori's LinkedIn Profile: _www.linkedin.com/in/LoriRuff_

Ed Redwood and his partner run a small Managed IT Company in London that employs a number of people and partners with other high-quality service providers to deliver value to their clients.

Here's Ed Redwood's LinkedIn Profile: _www.uk.linkedin.com/in/edredwood_

PrideStaff is a national staffing and recruiting company with company and franchise-owned stores. It is important for people in local markets to find the local stores, yet the company needs to promote and maintain their brand nationally. They have corporate employees, sales (to sell services), recruiters (to hire talent) and a variety of staffers who represent the company in the local workforce. Here are three of their profiles, two corporate and one franchisee:

Tammi Heaton's LinkedIn Profile: _www.linkedin.com/in/tammiheaton_

John-Reed McDonald's LinkedIn Profile: _www.linkedin.com/in/johnreedmcdonald_

Mike Eckelman's LinkedIn Profile: _www.linkedin.com/in/meckelman_

# Chapter Five

## Workin' for a living...

One thing that is different about each and every one of us is our work history. It's like a unique DNA. Many people have difficulty understanding what positions to include and, even harder, what to say about each of them. Strategies for doing both are covered here.

Sure, people have a presence on LinkedIn, but companies can play too! If fact, it's really easy to get a basic Company Page up on LinkedIn.

Be sure you don't use a personal profile to create a company presence. Talk about losing credibility quickly! Set up your own Personal Profile and your Company Page with the proper tools or people will wonder what you're trying to get away with... not the image you likely want to portray!

It is important to note that the main part of a LinkedIn Company Page isn't the "page" itself. It is the people, the employees associated with it. This gives your company credit for your stellar workforce; it looks more robust when you have a Rockstar team, no matter how large or small.

LinkedIn has built in lots of features that give LinkedIn Company Pages lots of interactive functionality that makes a difference in how people perceive you. This area is really evolving quickly.

Whether or not you own the company, correctly associating with your company on LinkedIn helps your credibility. Your mother probably told you that you are who your friends are. Well, she was right. The impression of the people who get to know you while reading your profile can be affected by who you work with or for.

There are some major elements that comprise the LinkedIn Company Page. First is the information you enter or someone at the organization enters (e.g. marketing). The second is the employees that identify themselves with the company on LinkedIn.

The Company Page on LinkedIn opens to an Overview providing general information, a partial listing of employees, and public information (Location, website, etc). The Page can be customized to activate TABS for listing jobs (Careers), displaying what the Company sells (Products & Services) and, for the Company Page Admin, Company Page Analytics.

The amount of information you can enter and display to the public is growing. You can even play YouTube videos about your product or service!

## TIP

We often recommend that executives include who and how to contact on their team rather than putting their own contact information in this semi-public space.

## Employees and Company Pages

The Company Page shows each employee that has properly associated with the company on LinkedIn. It is commonplace for even the most insightful employees not to show up. When we help companies address their identity on LinkedIn, we provide a set of instructions to make sure their staff knows how to do it right to provide and receive the most benefit. See the Tip associated with this section for the major points.

Every member of the band is accounted for and, even though each has their own role, everyone is singing from the same sheet of music.

**How You're Connected**

**16** first-degree connections

**1** second-degree connection

**23** Employees on LinkedIn

See all ▶

*The LinkedIn Company Page shows "how you are connected", for example, this is the Integrated Alliances Company Page.*

## TIP

To associate yourself to the Company Page properly, use the following technique:

1. If you do not have the job listed:
2. From the Experience Section, select the small text link "Add Position".
3. In the company name field, start entering the company name.
4. Keep an eye on LinkedIn's suggestions.
5. Select the company from the list.
6. Not on the list? There may not be a LinkedIn Company profile setup.

If you already have the job listed, but are not showing on the Company Page:

1. Starting at the Edit Profile Screen, find the position and click edit.
2. Pick the "Change Company" option in the company name field
3. Re-enter the company name keeping an eye on the suggestions that LinkedIn provides.
4. Select the company from the list.
5. Not on the list? There may not be a LinkedIn Company profile setup.

NOTES:

1. If a Company Page has not been set up, when you add the new Company, LinkedIn will ask for the Website and Industry. In order to set up a Company Page, you must have a unique domain name.
2. If a Company Page is set up and it still doesn't show, reach out to LinkedIn for assistance.

# Been There, Done That - Where?

**Every paid, project, or volunteer position you enter is an opportunity to create relationships, display your business worthiness, and expand keywords to attract more clicks resulting in more business.**

Your Work Experience section isn't seen as the most fun so we'll make it very SIMPLE and a little exciting. Ever wish you could expand on your resume? Here's your chance to make your experience shine! Here you get 2,000 characters per position to highlight your experience and accomplishments and describe how your experience relates to what you're doing now.

A resume can be repurposed a bit in this section, but not word for word. If you have multiple resumes, they should all agree with this area, but it doesn't have to be a duplicate.

The first *Key* is entering all of the positions you have held, since college or as far back as you need to go in order to build a solid picture of your professional life. We provide a list of logical questions to answer about each position, one after another: Company-Products-Customers-Territories-Roles-Accomplishments.

Tell readers what made you special at each position, what lasting impact you had in the organization, and what difference you made to others, whether co-worker or client. How does that experience relate to what you are doing today? How does it help make you the perfect choice to help others now?

Experts look to the past to get a clearer view of the future. We've heard this before and it rings more true than ever in a time where classic rock helps sell everything from Cadillacs to mops.

Would there be an iPod without the Sony Walkman? Would there be a digital camera without the Polaroid? The future is often foretold by the past. Historians study the past. Business people look to the future.

New business relationships can be formed based on experiences from your past. The further back you go to include past employment, the better chance you have of rekindling old relationships, making new ones and the BETTER those relationships can become.

Isn't it a bonding experience talking about the good old days? This form of nostalgic reminiscing is a key ingredient in The LinkedIn Rockstars' "secret sauce". We look for common experiences in the past of others to help us relate to them now; it's a chance to speak from shared experience.

*"Old Days"* (Chicago, 1975) is a song Chicago plays over 100 times a year in concert. They make a great living on nostalgia, don't they? Mike saw Chicago play for the first time in 1975 with the Doobie Brothers opening at the University of Minnesota. (Thanks to Mike's dad, Dr. Bernie O'Neil for taking him to the show!) Chicago is still at it and Mike is still going to their shows, even once in the Front Row.

## Methodological Approach

LinkedIn lets you enter information about each of the positions you have held. You can put in as many positions as you like. We typically suggest you put them ALL into LinkedIn.

Again, each position is a way to build relationships with others: former co-workers, partners, customers, and acquaintances. You only get credit for what you tell people about. This is also a great way to get additional "real estate" for keywords and marketing-type language. For the most part, LinkedIn will prompt you for this information:

+ Company Name
+ Title
+ Location
+ Time Period
+ Description

Since you are using the LinkedIn Profile Worksheet (right?), this isn't hard at all to do from scratch. We have really worked hard to make sure the worksheet eases the process.

On the next page is the screen for adding a position. When you type in the name of the company, LinkedIn will try and match a company already in the system. If it appears, just highlight the company and press enter, LinkedIn fills in the Website, Industry, Size (# of employees) and "links" your profile with the Company Page.

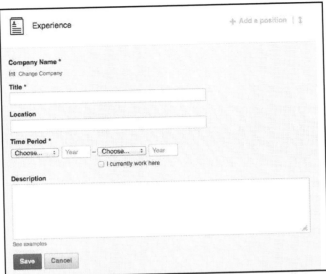

*Picking an employer properly from a drop-down list*

If the company name is not in the list, you can add it. If you have a company website, include it now. If no, no worries! Just fill in what you can.

Drilling down a bit deeper, we have some strategies, advice and best practices for you:

For most people, we recommend that you include all of your employers with major roles identified separately, significant projects if you are self-employed, and significant volunteer positions that either lend to your credibility and/or show experience you gained outside the workforce.

Be sure to check out the new Add Sections later in this book for tips about Projects, Organizations, and Volunteer Experience options. If you are able to obtain Recommendations for volunteer experience, we suggest you include that experience in the Experience Section since, at this time, you can't be recommended for work under the Add Sections options.

### Company Name

Your company name seems simple, and for most people it is. In business today it is commonplace to use abbreviations, variations and shortenings of the company name. Consider all of the options and do some searching on your own to see how others from the same company spell it. Use the most popular standard that you find to be sure you are properly affiliated with the LinkedIn Company Page if they have one.

## Time Period

The Time Period is just as it sounds and it is important for two particular reasons: the LinkedIn Colleagues feature and Reference Searches, both of which you will learn about later. Just include the years employed when LinkedIn asks you for the start and end dates.

Keep it simple. When the ordering of positions is not as you might like it, you may choose to add the month data to help in ordering. Job seekers can use months if they feel the need to. But read on: there are new options for reordering positions within your Experience!

## Ordering Positions

Positions are listed by current then past in order of start date. Those of you who read our first book know that, at that time, you could only reorder positions by fudging the start dates and including "ACTUAL DATES = xx-xx" at the top of the position description.

But LinkedIn finally caught on and now you have the ability to drag and drop positions within the Experience section and they will reorder in the Header as well. *WOOT! Way to go LinkedIn!*

## Job Titles

Feel free to show yourself in the best possible light: Sr. Account Executive sounds a lot better than Sales Rep. Just ensure the words you chose accurately represent your title and your role at the company.

You have 100 characters for the Job Title field and that's a lot. The LinkedIn Rockstars suggest you include acronyms and variations of your title to make it easier for people to find you.

For example, you might include "VP | Vice President", or "Sales Representative; Account Manager; Business Relationship Manager."

We ***strongly recommend*** that you supplement a formal job title with what that means for the reader. In other words, rather than just listing *"Account Executive"*, be more descriptive of the solution you offer or the people you serve, i.e., *"Account Executive | Consumer Products | Midwest Region."* This immediately lets viewers of your profile know if you're the person to help them, or if you can at least point them in the right direction.

## Multiple positions at the same company

If this is you and the positions were in different areas, put the job in twice (yes, as two independent jobs at the same company, but in a series.)

If the positions were in the same area and are more like a job progression (promotion), only list the highest position you held in the area (i.e., show Sales Manager vs. Sales Rep. AND Sales Manager.)

## Position Description

The more recent positions should have most of the following information included. More explanation than a bulleted list of your accomplishments is in order. Each position allows you 2,000 characters.

It can be hard to stare at a blank box wondering: "what do I put in now". It's even harder for people that have a lot of positions to do this multiple times.

## We'll make it SIMPLE. For each job, add the following information:

- ◆ What does the company do (what they make, sell, etc.)?
- ◆ Who do they do it for; who are their customers, especially if it isn't obvious (industry, type of account, functional level)?
- ◆ Where do THEY or YOU do it if it isn't obvious, i.e., regional, national, etc? *This is enhanced with the new "location" field, but that field indicates your location more than the company's.*
- ◆ What is/was your role?
- ◆ List anything important from a previous position that relates to what you do today. In other words, what made you special?
- ◆ Describe something amazing that you did or that happened when you were there. This is a great place to tell a short success story.

Make it exciting and stick to important facts, but do NOT overuse statistics like you might on a resume. Few people care if you were 221% of quota in 1998. They do want to know if you did international work or led a division or region or if you had a staff of X number of people reporting to you.

Rather than a bulleted list of accomplishments, "explore the space" and tell a story. It's much easier to read if you write as if you are describing the position in an interview.

## Concurrent Jobs

If you have or had a side business, put it in as a job, perhaps a "concurrent job." As described earlier, as you insert dates, LinkedIn will automatically order the positions according to start date. So, if you want to make your primary job prominent, just drag and drop it in the top position. It will reorder the jobs in your header as well.

*"Are you experienced?"* (Jimi Hendrix, 1967)

Is there something OTHER than traditional jobs that you might include? You can include other related work experiences. People want multi-dimensional partners, vendors, or employees nowadays. You want to show your skills and this is a great place to do it (as is the dedicated "Skills section" that follows.)

**Special Note to Job Seekers**

Keep in mind, that no matter what you put in your LinkedIn Profile, the information MUST agree with your resume (or resume versions) if you are a job seeker. Recruiters and HR professionals are looking to exclude people and a mis-match is enough to miss out.

Even though it must agree, it doesn't mean your profile has to be barren. People expect to see more information in your profile than in your one or two page resume. Be descriptive and use the space to give as complete a picture of your experience and expertise as you can!

Don't include a position stating you are Unemployed at Unemployed! Anything along those lines makes you look desperate and worse, incompetent.

You are a professional with skills, attributes, and knowledge who will make a great addition to the right team. Instead of focusing on what you aren't doing, focus on what you are doing to keep your skills sharp while you look.

**Quick Start for the "Most Experienced"**

If you want to truly FAST START the process and have an electronic resume, then use the existing resume text for now. People with lots of work experience may get the most out of this approach.

You must have an electronic version of your resume to effectively use this approach. As you add positions to your LinkedIn Profile, you can Copy/Paste the resume text section by section (job by job).

DO NOT use the resume important tool provided by LinkedIn. It's harder to clean up the oddball things it generates than it's worth at this point.

The idea is to get some basic job information in your profile and get on with the rest of it. You must go back and refine it eventually, but the process and momentum continues. Lay a good foundation now and keep working on it periodically, perhaps quarterly, to make it better.

# Chapter Six

## What you learned along the way...

There is education and then there is "LinkedIn education". There is a lot more to your education than just college, especially on LinkedIn. Most adults have learned in a number of ways over the years, in a number of places, using a number of means. Here we explore the different education to include and what to say about each.

# Education, Learning and More

**There is a lot more to education than a college degree, particularly continuing education and professional development; and it is all fair game. Show yourself to be a life-long learner.**

Here is another area where you can reuse a bit of your resume material but it doesn't stop there. Even if you didn't finish official schooling or just took a few classes, this information belongs in your LinkedIn Profile. But don't worry; there are some really good strategies for covering up any holes.

There are ways to ignore or build this section that won't hurt your credibility should you have no formal post-secondary education, or even if you didn't finish high school. There are a lot of successful people out there who are in the same boat. We know: they ask us what to do!

List the schools you attended all the way back to high school, to *"My Old School"* (Steely Dan, 1973), as it gives you another place to create bonds with other people. This technique even helps when you are building your LinkedIn network and inviting others.

Don't worry. If you aren't comfortable adding your high school, it's not required. Some people don't include it because it "ages" them. Others don't think it's relevant. Some didn't finish. But you don't have to include the years. That's not a required field. And if the alma matter network at your school is a strong one, we'd say why not rather than ask why.

Don't discount other forms of education either: professional development training, for example. *"I Know a Little"* (Lynyrd Skynyrd, 1974) adds up to a lot in the minds of others. People LOVE people with current skills and current knowledge, don't they?

Which is more important: Mike's Industrial Engineering degree from 1983 or the 3-day Social Media Conference he attended in 2011? It depends on the reader's point of view. But when you consider his specialty, the conference becomes more important, or at least begins to carry more weight.

The Education section is another area where your LinkedIn profile looks a bit like a resume. We suggest that you list all of your schools, including high school. If you went for two semesters or more, list it. If you took specialized classes that are relevant to what you do today, list them too. Dale Carnegie? Sure, include it. What else is there?

If you did anything special at these institutions, say so. If you were in a fraternity, sorority, sport, special interest group... put it in. You have 500 characters in Activities and Societies and 1,000 for Additional Notes!

Talk about why your education is relevant to your expertise NOW. Pack the paragraphs with keywords that you would most like to be found on. Be interesting. How? Sharing your experiences allow others to recognize shared experiences that create common bonds that result in relationships that mean business. Make sense?

We highly suggest that you do this for every educational experience. Even if you took one class or seminar at a college; adding it will allow you to join LinkedIn Alumni Groups.

*"School's out"* (Alice Cooper, 1972) doesn't mean that education is out. There are lots of vocational trainings, business trainings, LinkedIn trainings, conferences that make for good candidates here.

So, let's get some education on the profile, shall we?

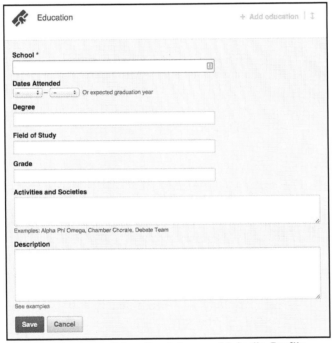

*Entering your Education into your LinkedIn Profile*

There are a few strategies that you can use to get the most out of education.

## School Name

Like elsewhere on LinkedIn (e.g., Adding a Position), you can simply start typing and LinkedIn will show you a list of matches. If your school is listed, by all means pick it. If not, you can add it in. *This is the only required field for this section.*

## Degree

While you can only see 20 characters at a time, you actually have a whopping 100 characters to work with. That is enough to put in a full degree name like "BS Industrial Engineering and Management Systems" or even something much larger. Just don't use any more characters than you need or it can be difficult for viewers to read.

## Field(s) of Study

If you had other significant areas that you studied, put them in here. Some examples might be "International Trade" or "Discreet Electronics."

## Dates Attended

Like the job dates, this is relatively significant. LinkedIn has a feature called Classmates that matches you up with other people you went to school with at the same time.

Some people have put in their educational experience and left off the dates so they could search for other alumni without being restricted by the years of their own attendance. If you are worried that the dates you were in school might age you, don't be. LinkedIn is full of middle aged and older people looking for others who have mature business careers. And, like Lori, there are many non-traditional college students out there.

## Activities and Societies Subsection

If you were part of any group (fraternity, sorority, clubs, sports, etc.) put this information here separated by commas.

**Hot Links**

The commas indicate the start and stop of a clickable keyword. Each word or phrase you enter here becomes a hotlink to an instant search within LinkedIn IF THE COMMAS ARE PUT IN PROPERLY. Simply enter the words and phrases separated by commas like this:

Phi Theta Kappa, Honor Society, graduated Cum Laude, Chess Club, Students Against Drunk Driving, GPA 3.96

To understand how this works, enter the information. Then go to "View Your Profile." You will see that all of these words and phrases are hotlinks so that, when you click them, LinkedIn performs a search of that keyword or phrase and allows you to find other people with the same word or phrase in their profile. If no one else comes up in the search, try modifying the information until you find other people. It doesn't help you much to stand alone here.

This is also a great way to search for other users with whom you already have something in common (connect with them!), as well as to be more findable when others perform those searches too.

**Additional Notes**

Was there anything especially noteworthy about your experience? Put it here. This is a good place to tell a story about why you picked the major or industry focus that you did. Also, why your education proved to be relevant to the work you do now.

If your education was quite a while ago, you might start with something like: "I didn't realize it at the time, but..." The point is, you have 1,000 characters to work with here, so pack the space with more keywords that will allow people to find you through your profile by searching LinkedIn, and with a story that will allow readers of your profile to understand you better or to connect with you through shared experiences.

# Your 15 Minutes of Fame

**Toot your horn, go for it, this is why you tried so hard in the first place! Let others know which achievements mean the most to you.**

Are you famous for anything, even in very small circles? Don't we all have our 15 minutes of _"Fame"_ (David Bowie, 1975)? If you won an award or were recognized, say so. President's club, employee of the month, Sales Rep of the Year, public speaking appearances, being #1 at something... you get the idea. Especially if you were recognized by your peers, include it here.

Most people have SOMETHING that was special, something for which they were recognized. No honors and awards police will come knocking, but don't fib just to put something here. If you were #1 at one point, say so.

It is NOT required that you list anything. If you leave it empty, the field just doesn't show. It won't leave a glaringly blank section on your profile.

If you have any notable honors or awards, by all means mention them if you think the people you are trying to attract will look favorably upon them. Others may search on that particular search term and you will come up. Be proud of your honors, show them!

This is also a great place to identify Professional Credentials that are related to your job, but not tied to one in particular.

# Chapter Seven

## Your Personal side...

Much of LinkedIn, for the most part, a relatively pure business platform. There are select places where you can effectively share a bit about your personality. It's even further down in your profile and it includes your Interests, Organizations you associate with, "advice for contacting you" and, for some, what you have going on (status updates).

_"Walk this way"_ (Aerosmith, 1975)

We like to call this the Facebook Section of your LinkedIn Profile. It's a sort of organized catchall section for those little things that don't get their own region. Frankly, The LinkedIn Rockstars feel these are among the most important areas, especially when engaging others.

If you want powerful business relationships with people you really enjoy, with people that really enjoy you, share some things about yourself. YOU put in the words that bring you together with others that you really enjoy. You don't have to disclose anything you're not comfortable with, but share something that you might talk about over a beer to help people get to know you better.

The Additional Information section of LinkedIn is the place to do that. It is by default located near the bottom of your LinkedIn Profile. Two parts—your Web sites and your Twitter ID's—also appear in the Header Area at the top.

The data you are asked for in the Additional Information Area include:

**Interests** – what you LIKE to do, mostly personal, but you can include additional professional and/or educational interests.

**Groups & Associations** – who you associate with, business and personal, and consider including the groups & associations of customer groups. (We cover more on this later...)

**Honors & Awards** – special accomplishments and recognition. We all prefer to do business with interesting people don't we? All else being equal, isn't it better to do business with people we like? LinkedIn groups a suite of fields together under the title "Additional Information." It is the often best place to find information that helps us build lasting, meaningful relationships.

*"Like to get to know you well"* (Howard Jones, 1984)

The LinkedIn summary is perhaps our favorite and the most useful section of the entire LinkedIn Profile. Use the information contained here to speak to the person, to the individual, and not to the employee or to the worker. Look to this section to get to better know people before reaching out to them. Our business calls go great as a result. Yours will too.

Some of our best relationships with new friends have started by finding LinkedIn connections who built this section out. We were excited to meet them for the first time, and once we did, we were excited at the chance to do business together. The music we create now sounds sweeter because of it! One of our best friends, Steven Groves, co-author of ROI of Social Media, is just such a relationship, as are many others.

Heck, we even met on LinkedIn when Lori did a search for professionals in Denver that included Mike. They exchanged messages, talked on the phone and knew doing business together would be brilliant.

What if our friends and people we meet could tell us about all of their interests? We'd learn a lot we didn't know. The same goes for people we work with, those we meet in business. You get the idea. Relationships are built on shared experiences, friendships more so. Give people an opportunity to realize they would ENJOY you as a person... you might even be FUN to do business with. Isn't that a great tie-breaker?

The Additional Information sections are a medley that makes this kind of bonding possible, perhaps along the lines of *"A Day in the Life"* (The Beatles, 1967): it's a nice assortment of things that could be sections on their own, but group together very well.

**On the Offense**

We make HUGE use of the Interests section. Whenever we are preparing to contact someone new, we head right here. We want to know what we might discover after a few beers together but we want that information going in.

We want to know what they like for fun, what professional associations and organizations they align themselves with, whether they are businesslike or perhaps more informal or family oriented. Do they live a balanced life? You can tell a lot here and it isn't hard if it's completed well.

# Connect with LinkedIn Interests

**Showing others who you are like as a real person, off hours, will draw people in that you can really "click" with in business too.**

Interests is our #1 most favorite field on ALL of LinkedIn both to share ourselves with other people and to glean information about people we're about to meet. It works both ways.

Mike gets to show people _"The real me"_ (The Who, 1973) and Lori shows her _"True colors"_ (Cyndi Lauper, 1986). Here, people get to be people, not just employees and business professionals.

Done right, it works very well; done wrong there can be some minor problems. Explore the space provided! Look what other people you respect are doing and mimic their efforts. But make it personal and keep it fresh.

Here you can share your LIKES – what you like to do, like to listen to, like to watch, like to buy. For the most part, it's about things you do ON YOUR OWN TIME, not on the company clock.

**What can you share that others might also be passionate about?**

   ◆ Movies, music, hobbies, travels? YES.
   ◆ Dislikes, turnoffs, your wild side? NO.

Why do the LinkedIn Rockstars give so much attention to Interests? LinkedIn is a business tool, right?

**Is it personal or is it business?**

When you share an interest with someone else, the relationship starts off on the right foot. You show more interest in THEM and less in their POSITION. It doesn't take long for business to creep into the conversation if you start out on a personal note with someone new.

It's like targeted marketing and selling. In theory, a niche gets you more qualified prospects and gets your clients more qualified vendors. The Repair shop vs. the Acura-Honda Repair shop. If I'm driving an Acura TL with that electronic instrument panel, I know which repair shop I'm taking my car to.

Now turn the table. Others feel that way too. This is what makes business fun, it brings perks too. Perhaps an example or two...

If Mike were interested in the ballet, he would put it his profile. But he's not so he puts in classic bands like PINK FLOYD, The Eagles, John Mellencamp, Tom Petty instead.

## Perks Are Better with Business Partners/Friends

In a business world where tickets are passed around, Mike would much prefer that ticket to Red Rocks vs. the Ballet. Our friend Ben Goss in Denver knows this. He's been to Mike's LinkedIn Profile and our training sessions and he knows what we like. Ben has shared tickets to events he couldn't attend with us, really nice tickets to concerts and sporting events. We LOVE Ben for that and provide help and advice for him as well.

Our relationship is one where we bring value to each other. Ben gets professional help, we get a night out. It's a win-win for all! This relationship enabled Mike to take his 12 year-old son Brendan to see 3 Dog Night play a summer show in the Colorado Mountains, front row no less.

_"All I want to do"_ (Sheryl Crow, 1994)

Interests and business perks work even better for sporting events, where company-owned and individual-owned season tickets are always floating around. If people know you are interested in say the Colorado Avalanche, you are closer to going to a free game and that means dinner and drinks in many cases.

Remember YOU can be THEIR key to going to the game or the show. It's a perk for THEM too. While this isn't what it used to be when entertainment money really flowed, it's still a common practice and the Interests section helps with a LOT.

We also know who of our friends and business partners like what kind of shows so when we have plans to go, we let them know so there's an opportunity for us to go together... shared experience. That's what builds relationships!

## Sorting It Out

The information entered in the Interests Section tends to fall into 3 basic camps:

1. What we pay money to buy or do. Skiing, travel, boating, records.
2. What we enjoy doing naturally, perhaps "free things". Hiking, exercise, dogs, cats, alligators.
3. Preferences like favorite bands, movies, TV shows, etc.

The bottom line is this: what are you passionate about?

This area is where LinkedIn is light years behind Facebook and probably always will be. Don't be discouraged. This is a professional environment. But we are about to share some best practices and secrets for bringing you more and better professional relationships using common interests to help you find people you will enjoy doing business with!

## Inspiration

Let others see the things that inspire you, the things you LIKE – what you like to do, like to see, like to hear... what you choose to spend personal time and discretionary income on. Paint a picture of what you're like to be around. It really helps create new relationships with others, all within comfortable surroundings.

## Things You Like

We all like THINGS. Mention muscle cars, classic rock, Colorado and you have our attention. What gets you excited? In this context, kids and family might be the ticket. You'll see more in the examples coming up.

## Activities You Like

These are personal interests for the most part (golf, skiing, traveling, Little League Baseball, etc.) Be specific: Downhill Skiing or Slalom rather than just skiing. List in the order of what is most important to you, group them as appropriate. In this, kids and family might show more as ACTIVITIES.

## Formatting

Be sure to list the words or phrases separated by commas. Each word or phrase becomes a clickable link to others on LinkedIn that share that particular "keyword or phrase", but only IF THE COMMAS ARE PUT IN PROPERLY. Remember, you only see the links as others will see them in the "View My Profile" mode, not in "Edit" mode.

This LinkedIn section supports special characters that help make it interesting. For example Mike uses Musical notes, a TV icon and the like to break it up and attract attention. It really works.

When we tell others about what we like, perks as well as personal conversations are more focused in those areas. It's only natural.

Mike finds that he often has a Mountain Dew waiting for him nowadays when he speaks or trains. People who do their homework on their guests, like Colorado Springs radio show hosts Ted Robertson and Joanna Hoiberg, are the masters at this research. Score!

Used properly, the Interests Section can truly be a secret weapon. Instead of agonizing over how to engage someone, you examine his or her INTERESTS. Vice versa, you hang your interests out there for others to engage. It definitely triggers action if done right.

Here are some good examples from RockTheWorld clients:

**Interests**
Surfing, car racing, skiing, reading, playing bridge, and writing

**Interests**
My teenage daughter, Horse back riding, Mounted Patrol of San Mateo County, Healthy cooking, hiking, biking, Pilates, gardening, rural life, emerging technologies, usability research, sustainable energy

**Interests**
MUSIC, concerts, Pink Floyd, Counting Crows, Tom Petty, ACTIVITIES, car shows, movies, travel, Mexico, TECHNOLOGY, iPhone, iPad,Apple Store, CARS, Corvette, Camaro, Ferrari, TV, The Family Guy, Boston Legal, Seinfeld

And Mike's Interests which shows the field fully used (1,000 characters) and using special characters:

**Interests**
♫ I enjoy live music, concerts, classic rock, Pink Floyd, Steely Dan, Tom Petty, U2, Didgeridoo, Hammond B3 FUN, I play pool & foosball, watch football & hockey, have dogs & cats, drink Heineken, Stella Artois, Mountain Dew, sleep OWN, I love Apple products and the Apple store, vinyl records, Band & Olufson turntable, tech gadgets, MOVIES, I love Almost Famous, Forrest Gump, Office Space, TV, I watch Steven Colbert, The Family Guy, The Simpsons, SNL, CARS, I love classic cars & muscle cars e.g. Corvette, Camaro, Mustang, Shelby, Ferrari, Aston Martin, Duesenberg, DeLorean.

# Those Additional Organizations

**Where you practice professional business socializing can bring you closer to just the right people for you.**

Note that this is the text area for listing Groups and Associations, not where you select which LinkedIn Groups to join. Carefully selecting the right Groups and Associations, both here and in the LinkedIn Groups Section, will add greatly to your LinkedIn and business credibility. It lets THEIR good brand reflect on YOU a bit. It also allows you to exhibit the time and effort invested in areas mentioned throughout your profile as important to you. It helps you create consistency, which builds trust.

Picture a concert now - doesn't the opening band enjoy credibility shared from the show's headliner? Of course! In fact, the opening act may return soon as the main attraction.

The words you include here are the names of the groups along with their acronyms separated by commas. Again here, the simple text in this section directly follows the Interests section. Again, this is NOT the LinkedIn Groups that have attractive little icons, discussions, and members you can message.

When formatted correctly, People who click on groups here will be led to search results of other LinkedIn users that list the same organization in THEIR profiles.

Our most frequent question in this category – do you have to be a member of the groups to list them? NO you do not! But you should have some affiliation. For example, you're not a CPA, but many of your clients are. List groups they belong to as groups you serve.

If you are a member of any professional associations or groups, you definitely want to include them here. Enter the full name, followed by a comma, followed by any acronyms or abbreviations the organization uses, followed by a comma and repeat over and over.

This is a great place to think back to previous groups that you might have been a part of, perhaps even in other cities. You are trying to put hooks out there to reconnect with people from your past. This is one method.

Non-profits and charitable causes are great to list. Others will be especially interested in seeing this side of you.

## Formatting – The Comma

As with the Interests section and elsewhere, each word or phrase you enter here and separate them with commas, will show you others that list the same word or phrase in their profiles.

For example: *American Society for Training & Development, ASTD.* Both American Society for Training & Development, and ASTD are clickable hot links. Also notice that we chose the ampersand "&" rather than spelling out the word "and." To the LinkedIn search engine, "and" and the ampersand are now interchangeable and space matters so choose the version with less characters.

**TIP**

As you complete each section of your profile, look at "View My Profile" to see how other LinkedIn users will see it. Also do searches on the hot linked words and phrases to see what comes up.

If you find few matches you may consider an alternative word or phrase. Put the words and phrases with a poor match (only a handful of results) somewhere else and save this sacred hot links section for words and phrases that will help you be found in more common searches.

## Membership?

You do NOT need to be a member of a group or association to list it. There should be some level of affiliation, but it can be just "I follow this group" to be able to accurately list it in your profile. Again, this is different from being a "member" of a true LINKEDIN GROUP.

Give some thought to anything that might be controversial with respect to your target audience on LinkedIn. The National Rifle Association, NRA, is one example where you may have to give it some thought. But, if it makes sense, use it as it creates online, searchable bonds with other NRA members.

If it is a group that is important to you, you might also see if they have a full-blown LinkedIn Group that you could join. That would be IN ADDITION to listing it here.

# Sharing "Personal Information"

**Your direct connections should see every way to reach you: That's Cool! Don't hide from the people who want to bring business to you!**

When you make yourself more available, more opportunities come your way. *"Call me"* (Blondie, 1980) is what many of us want our viewers to do. Along that vein, a phone number and a physical area or email address that others can see will help you realize greater results with LinkedIn. This is an obvious fact is too often overlooked.

Most of the information you enter in the Personal Information section is ONLY viewable by your direct Tier 1 connections.

For that reason it is used in concert with the Contact Settings field, duplicating some of the data. Neither field shows to the outside world who might view your public profile; rather only when people are actually logged into LinkedIn.

Here is the place that LinkedIn would like you to officially put your phone number, instant messaging service, address, birthday, and marital status for your network to see.

The settings allow you to enter one phone number (home, work or mobile), one instant-messaging service (AIM, Skype, Windows Live Messenger, Yahoo! Messenger, ICQ, or GTalk), your address, birthday, birth year, and marital status.

We don't enter any information for Birthday, Year or Marital Status but for different reasons. For Lori it is a privacy issue, but she loves to celebrate so she shows April 12 in the Birthday field.

Notice in the screen shot how she handles the address field: the intension gives people an idea of where they can find us. Mike lists a PO Box address.

**Advice for Contacting Michael**  ✎ Edit

---

**Advice for people who want to contact you**

> I am open connecting if it makes sense (and it usually does). I can be reached at 303-683-9600 anytime or via E-Mail at mpatrick@IntegratedAlliances.com.

Anything you add here — including contact info — could be visible to people who view your profile.

---

*Personal Information Section Example*

For Mike it's a formatting issue. He places the Personal Information Section above his Summary.

Our dear friend and privacy and security expert Winn Schwartau includes "Married". He explained on our radio show *RockTheWorld with LinkedIn* (*www.RockTheWorldRadio.com*) that its public information anyway so he's fine sharing it here.

As you enter your information, notice that there is a tiny blue lock beside Birthday, Birth Year, and Marital Status. Just as with your maiden/former name field, this lock allows you to choose whether to show these fields to My Connections (Tier 1 connections only), My Network (Tier 1, 2, 3 connections, and group members) or to Everyone (all of the hundreds of millions of people on LinkedIn).

Which is right for you? You need to decide now so you can participate later already understanding where your chosen limits are.

**Want a peek behind the scenes?**

*Entering data into the Personal Information section*

# LinkedIn Network Updates

**Network Updates is a LinkedIn tool that populates your LinkedIn homepage, helping you keep an eye on what your direct connections are up to.**

*"Stayin' alive"* (The Bee Gees, 1977)

LinkedIn has a terrific feature called Network Updates. It is how your connections can follow what you are up to: Profile changes, Profile additions, Status Updates and more. This service may need to be enabled in your LinkedIn Settings.

You can see this feature in action on your own LinkedIn Home Page. Go there and you can take a peek at what your Tier 1 connections are up to as well. Use this to respond and engage people in your network. See something interesting? Reach out!

Your LinkedIn Home Page shows a stream of updates from your Tier 1 connections. As a new update is made from these individuals, it goes on the top of the list and pushes the others down. That's what we mean by a stream. It works both ways. When you make updates to your profile, others will be notified in the Network Updates "stream" on their LinkedIn Home Page too.

People see these and other updates and they reach out to you. Don't be surprised when someone says they *"Heard it through the grapevine"* (Marvin Gaye, 1968) and they called to you as a result. It's happened to us and others, it can happen for you too!

### Why Updates Matter

From a marketing sense, it's good to get yourself in front of others. It's the "more is better principle". Network Updates is a great way to "drip market" yourself to your tier 1 and, as described above, your tier 2 connections.

They see you are active, doing things and being inspiring. Some people will find that interesting. You can expect to see your Profile Views (by others) increase as you do things that trigger network updates.

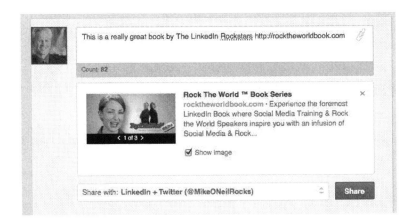

*Change your LinkedIn Status Update from your Home Page*

Sex it up a bit by adding a link. Enter a YouTube video URL and it will play RIGHT IN YOUR PROFILE. By entering a URL, you will be presented with more places to put attractive text. Take advantage of all of these features to get the most out of LinkedIn Status Updates.

# Updating Your Profile

**After you build out your LinkedIn Profile, you will see more things that inspire you to come back to make changes to your own profile and that is GREAT! Stay inspired, stay current, stay on top.**

In your newly energized LinkedIn endeavors (hopefully due to reading this book) you will see new things as you peruse other people's profiles: you'll discover new words, notice new concepts and gather new recommendations. You will want to incorporate these new ideas into your profile. PLEASE DO! Not only will it keep you ahead of the game, but it will also notify your Tier 1 connections in their Network Updates stream of the changes you make and keep you top of mind.

In the world of online media, it's about _"Changes"_ (David Bowie, 1974) and it is very similar to web site SEO, a process that usually has a lot of upfront work to get to solid long-lasting results.

When you keep your LinkedIn Profile up-to-date, it shows others that you are engaged, that you are currently in the game. It is like seeing a blog that has been updated in the last week vs. one that was last updated six months ago. We know which we prefer and we know who more often than not gets the deal.

As you see more and more of other people's profiles, you will get more and more ideas about what you can adopt for use in your own profile. A keyword, an adjective, some special characters, or something else that attracted YOU to THEM might attract OTHERS to YOU. No one person or place has all of the ideas nor do they have all the creativity so keep reading, keep searching, keep "exploring the space."

Early on while creating your presence on LinkedIn, learn all you can from as many sources as you can find, look at as many profiles as you can, make lots of notes, and then compile the best of them for use in YOUR LinkedIn Profile.

Each time you make these updates, others will see that you have something new, something current going on in your professional life and you will once again rise up to the top of their list, to the top of their minds.

In case you didn't start at the beginning of the book, to begin editing your LinkedIn Profile, simply hover over the Profile menu and select the Edit Profile menu item.

**Network Update Triggers**

1. Making changes to your LinkedIn Profile

   Update a section; change a picture; add a URL: they are all in the same camp. LinkedIn will let your Tier 1 connections know that you have made the change and provide a link to your profile so they can see it.

2. Adding new positions, education, sections to your LinkedIn Profile

   When you make additions (vs. making changes listed above), LinkedIn will send a notice in your Network Updates and others that you have added important information to your profile. They will see it in their Network Updates stream. It will appear on Their Home Page when they go there. How's that for letting people know your career is rocking?

3. LinkedIn Status Updates

   From your LinkedIn Home Page you can make status updates that go right on your LinkedIn Profile. These updates are also placed in the steam your tier 1 connections see on their LinkedIn home pages. Also, if someone "Likes" or "Comment On" your status update, their connections see that activity in their streams. That means, via what Lori calls the "Power of the Overheard Word," many of your tier 2 connections will get a peek at what you are up to. (Another reason we recommend your updates are appropriate for the office water cooler conversation.)

**TIP**

The LinkedIn Status feature allows you to "Attach a link". When you do it finds a picture from the link to display, perhaps several to choose from even.

Knowing this, the formatting of the page at the URL can have a great impact on what others see and on turning profile traffic into business. Once you attach the link, you can edit the Title and Descriptive Text to further customize the messaging.

Keep in mind that the Title, Text, Image and/or Video must be consistent with what they will actually find at the site if you want to have happy visitors.

# Chapter Eight

## Twitter & Recommendations for Attention & Respect

LinkedIn has tight integration with Twitter and it is one way – out. This interface gets you attention as others see your post and respond. Recommendations get you the respect that comes from others telling your story. This chapter covers both and you will see how they relate to one another.

# Share What's "New" With LinkedIn Status Updates

**A LinkedIn Status Update is a marketing message nowadays; use it strategically, with a new update every 1-10 days.**

LinkedIn's Status field has counterparts in Twitter, Facebook and other platforms and it is tempting to address them all equally. However, your LinkedIn Status is NOT the same thing. LinkedIn is more static, more strategic, and *more business*.

We mean that! It doesn't have to be completely business, but it never something you would not say in a business environment. It might be what you mention at the water cooler or walking into a business meeting, at a networking event or with a colleague over lunch. By sharing those statements in a public environment, you can capture what Lori likes to call "the power of the overheard word."

Let's discuss this. Facebook and Twitter are more real-time, more about *"What's goin' on"* (Marvin Gaye, 1971): things get obsolete very quickly. They may or may not be about business matters. They are often in fact very personal.

Twitter is updated several times a day! If you connect your Twitter account to automatically update EVERY post to LinkedIn, imagine how quickly your colleagues—who may have less than a couple hundred connections—will become overwhelmed by your constant ranting. We have heard personally from people who got into trouble by over-communicating on LinkedIn in this way and needed help rebuilding their credibility. Remember, LinkedIn is a place to BUILD your reputation, not destroy it!

Your LinkedIn Status Updates, on the other hand, will indeed be about business, almost exclusively. This is a SUPER-POWERFUL FEATURE that is growing in importance every day.

*LinkedIn and Twitter can be connected but beware!*

LinkedIn suggests you "Share an update". Call it a *"Message in a bottle"* (The Police, 1979).

## But aren't they the same thing?

Again, at first glance they seem almost identical. LinkedIn says "Share an update" Twitter asks "What's happening?" It takes an expert to sort through all this and you will be particularly happy you bought this book for this one section.

|  | **LinkedIn** | **Twitter** |
|---|---|---|
| **Message Length** | 600 | 140 |
| **http:// Link Support** | Yes | Yes |
| **Hashtags supported** | Yes, to LinkedIn Signal | Yes |
| **@Name clicking support** | Yes, to Twitter | Yes |
| **Rich Media Support** | Yes | when viewing message |
| **Rich Media Description** | 100+ characters | No |

### Integrating LinkedIn and Twitter

LinkedIn offers 2-way integration between the LinkedIn Status and Twitter Updates. In other words, LinkedIn can update your Twitter Status and Twitter can be setup to update your LinkedIn Status. As we have already alluded to, there are significant issues to consider.

## How it all works

When you update your LinkedIn status, you have the option to have that same message "Tweeted" for you. Only the first 140 characters will show on Twitter. If you go over, the update will be truncated. Both support clickable links in the messages. That is where they are similar.

Here's where the differences between LinkedIn Status and Twitter Status start. The LinkedIn Rockstars are among the world's elite on Twitter as well. In the Twitter world, they recommend Status Updates (Tweets) be no longer than 110-120 characters.

Why not use all 140 characters you are allotted? In Twitter it is common for others to forward these messages (Re-Tweet) and this requires extra characters (20-30) to allow for the credit: for example, "RT @MikeONeilRocks".

In the LinkedIn Status Update, we recommend using as much space as you need to post a coherent and intelligent update that provides value for or makes an announcement to your network, perhaps something that reinforces your value statement. Forwarding is not supported in the same way so you don't need to reserve the Re-Tweet space.

Instead, people on LinkedIn, whether or not they are connected to you, can Like, Comment on, or Share your update. Most people will see your update when they are directly connected to you. However, once they Like or Comment, it shares that with their network too.

We have examples of people who saw a workshop or event that we would be at nearby because one of our connections, like Pink Floyd, said "Wish I could be there!" At least twice that we know of, this resulted in people attending our event. One of those people became a friend and vendor. How's that for an example of business results from a simple yet powerful tool?

Your LinkedIn Status also lets you attach a clickable link to your update. It even shows a nice media-rich preview of the URL location and pulls some text and pictures from the site. A YouTube link is golden: it plays the video right in the status window without ever leaving LinkedIn!

Do you see all the extra capabilities; all the options; all the power?

So, what actually happens when you update your LinkedIn Status?

Your LinkedIn Status appears in the most prime space on your LinkedIn Profile: in the header below your Name/Headline/Location/Industry. This information is seen by people that view your profile (unless you have it set not to, but if your idea is to promote, why would you do that?). The LinkedIn Status Update can do a lot more for you however.

When you update your LinkedIn Status, a notification goes out to your Tier 1 connections in the Network Updates on their home page. They have the opportunity to see your new update and have links back to your profile included.

Again, people can Like, Comment on, or Share your update, which sends it out to their connections network updates... are you starting to see the potential here for people to "overhear" the conversation? By the way, the power of the Share on LinkedIn means you can share it with an individual, with a group, or you can post someone else's update to your own.

Why would you do that? Mike and Lori share each other's frequently, so can others on the same team. We also often will share the updates of people we respect when they have something cool happening that we think is important for our networks to know.

All this can bring you lot's of new opportunities, especially if you craft a really good status update.

### Status Strategies from the Marketing World

Introduce a new project you are working on. Every few days update the project with something interesting and insightful.

| Original message | "Just began a 12 site Voice Over IP (VOIP) telecom rollout for a new client. It's a dandy network that even integrates cell phones!" |
|---|---|
| Update 1 | Large telecom rollouts that rely on cell phones are not no-brainers as I'm discovering in a 12 site VOIP rollout." |
| Update 2 | "Clients sure are digging these new VOIP capabilities with integrated cell phones. My 12-site rollout is really shining; already getting new leads from the buzz!" |

# Get Recommended to get Respected

**What others say about you is 100 times more powerful than what you say about yourself; LinkedIn Recommendations are the perfect path to increasing your credibility.**

_"I get by with a little help from my friends"_ (The Beatles, 1967)

LinkedIn Recommendations show others you are business worthy. They help you "Back It Up" through third party personal testimonials that attest to something positive about your skills. It's not a Grammy, but it's in that league, especially in the credentials-loving LinkedIn world.

The best references are usually from customers, co-workers and superiors. Have them tell a 3-4 sentence "story" that highlights your impact on the success of a finite business project. You are not seeking a puff piece! Make sure they describe your WORK rather than your CHARACTER. It's ok to include both, but people want to know you can deliver. They can get what it might be like to actually work with you from the personality you infuse into other areas of your profile.

Recommendations are like References; they are Votes for you.

LinkedIn Recommendations can come in several varieties – character references (low value), school references (valuable in some instances), peer or co-worker references (valuable), project references (more valuable), client references (the MOST valuable of all). In any case, these must be true references in LinkedIn. Where you may not need to know someone to connect on LinkedIn, you MUST HAVE first-hand experience with them and/or their work to recommend them.

Call it integrity; call it best practices; call it spam-fighting; let's just call it the right thing to do. In order to request recommendations from within LinkedIn, you have to be connected.

The LinkedIn Rockstars have hundreds of LinkedIn recommendations (not all showing) from others that have experienced our work. Maybe they saw us speak, attended training, read the book, perhaps we helped them out. We provided value, they liked it, and they wrote a nice recommendation. Nice!

Nowadays our business and personal lives are as integrated as ever. Our co-workers become our friends, our neighbors help us find a job, the smart phone is always there as a bridge. Is the number of recommendations we have too many? Should you try to get hundreds too? Well, consider that we're in front of a lot of people. Sometimes we mention from the front of the class, "if you like our work, please recommend us!"

The number of recommendations you should seek depends on how many people you come into regular contact with in your job. According to LinkedIn, your profile is not "complete" until you have 3. We recommend most people seek 5-20… about one for each year of experience. For entry-level folks, those educational references and intern positions with associated recommendations are worth their weight in gold!

We get lots of questions about how to include Recommendations or testimonials on your LinkedIn Profile from other sources. You could use the Box.net application, or you could include pieces of testimonials in the position description, but those won't necessarily carry the same weight as actual LinkedIn Recommendations processed through the platform itself.

If you are not connected to a person you'd like a recommendation from, ask them to send a recommendation using your name and email address.

LinkedIn actually keeps score on Recommendations. You see the # of recommendations that are "shown" clearly displayed in the header of a profile. This assumes that all recommendations are the same and they are NOT.

**Case in point**

Mike worked in Telecom for many years as a Sales Engineer, quota and all. In the job he worked on projects with engineers that installed routers, people that sold the equipment, companies that financed the deals, the help desk managers, etc. They all contributed to the recommendations Mike now enjoys. They paint a picture that gets to look like a motion picture. But Mike is no longer a sales engineer? Isn't he? Does his work ethic and sense of delivering a job well done stop because he's focused on a new effort?

## Scoring Recommendations

To make it more helpful to you as you gather recommendations, we developed a scoring system so you can focus your efforts and begin to build diversity in your recommendations. We score it from 1 to 5 points.

**1 Pointers**

Friends that recommend one another on LinkedIn, pure character references. C-mon, *"You've got a friend"* (James Taylor, 1971) is a great song but it is not a great premise for a LinkedIn Recommendation.

A few of these are OK to have, but it takes a lot of pennies to buy anything and people don't pay attention to pennies much anymore. They want to know that someone is fun and interesting to be around, but not at the expense of more meaningful business references. Don't let character reference hide "higher point" references.

**2 Pointers**

References from school and education references. If the association was recent or it was an Executive MBA program or if education carries more importance that normal in your field, these will have more meaning. Perhaps they are 3 or 4 pointers for you.

**3 Pointers**

Are from co-workers or others that you worked with. They paint a picture of what it was like to work with you. This might be as a peer at the same company, peers at different companies or perhaps a level or two up or down the corporate ladder from you.

**4 Pointers**

Projects! Here people had a chance to experience your work first hand. They were there as well; they had skin in the game. Many of the things they may say about you might be true in reverse as well. We'll come back to that in a moment. If you want people to BUY from you or HIRE you, these are especially powerful.

**5 Pointers**

Are from the eye of the customer. What do the people who give you their money say about that experience? Sales professionals should focus the most attention here, especially for recent positions.

## How many Recommendations is enough?

There is much to debate, but The LinkedIn Rockstars feel you should aim for 5 to 20 recommendations. Think of it as 1 per year of professional experience with exceptions at both the low and high end of the scale. You might also consider how much exposure you have to a variety of people. If you work in a small office with little customer contact, just a few recommendations is fine.

Recommendations are associated with specific positions you entered or with specific educational institutions you entered. They are not about YOU, but your performance at one of these entities. It has a home base on your profile.

## An example:

> "Mike led a project where we brought up telecom services for 8 offices over a long weekend. His hard work and expert planning allowed the project to go off without a hitch. We simply couldn't have done it without him. I highly recommend Mike if you want complex conversions done right!"

Try to keep them to three to five sentences in length and suggest that to others as well. Recommendations from individuals with higher-level job titles (President, VP, etc.), even at small companies, are the great sources of recommendations. Seek at least a few of these.

Another great resource for recommendations is individuals who work for well-known companies (household names). People are impressed that Lori provides excellent training, for some reason they are even more impressed to know she provided excellent training for AT&T. Perhaps the difficulty of landing a training gig with AT&T carries more weight than training the local small business office. In other words, if you have worked for someone people respect, a recommendation from that source will carry more weight.

## Getting started with LinkedIn Recommendations

It all starts from the Profile TAB at the left, where it fits nicely. LinkedIn Recommendations are an integral part of LinkedIn Profiles aren't they? This will lead you to 3 options and they all have to do with getting and managing Recommendations.

*Getting to the LinkedIn Recommendations area*

# Managing Recommendations

When you start getting LinkedIn Recommendations, it won't be long before you need to manage them. Some recommendations will be better than others. You don't have to display all your LinkedIn Recommendations, but you do need to display enough.

**So, here's a decent roadmap.**

- ♦ Request more than you need (30)
- ♦ To get enough (20), so you can
- ♦ Select the best to display (15)
- ♦ Have enough good recommendations in the end (10-15)

In the LinkedIn Management screen, you'll see each of your positions and educational experiences with links to help you manage your recommendations.

If you have Received Recommendations for a position, you will see the total number of recommendations for that position, how many you have made visible, how many are hidden, and how many pending requests you have.

**Make a recommendation**

At the bottom, you have a form available to "Make a recommendation." You simply put in the first and last name, the email, and then indicate whether you are recommending the person as a Colleague, Service Provider, Business Partner or Student. Click "Continue."

If the recommendation is for a Service Provider, complete a form to indicate the position you're recommending the person for, the service category, the year first hired. A checkbox indicates if you've hired this person more than once. Also choose three attributes from a list to describe the person you are recommending.

If it is for a colleague, business partner, or student, you have different options.

For a colleague or student, you will select the basis for the recommendation. That is, what was your relationship to this person?

- ♦ For a colleague, was this a direct reporting relationship, or did you work with them in the same or a different group?
- ♦ For students, were you their teacher, or advisor, or did you study with them?
- ♦ Next you will select your title and the other person's title (select each of these options from drop-down menus) "at the time" you knew them, which will be the period covered by your recommendation.

Now, you have to actually write a concise yet descriptive recommendation.

Finally, you will see a link at the bottom to [view/edit] a message to be sent with your recommendation. "I've written this recommendation of your work to share with other LinkedIn users." This text is OK to leave, but you may want to personalize the message and then click "send."

You will see a message: "Your (type) recommendation has been created" at the top of your screen.

Recommendations you make or receive are shown on your member feed and on the network update of your connections. Once accepted, it will show on their Member Activity and Network Updates as well.

On the Recommendations Screen, in the bar entitled "Recommendations," you will notice there are three tabs: Received Recommendations, Sent Recommendations, and Request Recommendations.

The "Received Recommendations" tab is highlighted.

Click on "Sent Recommendations" to see the listing of recommendations you have sent. You can filter the list by type; you can edit each, and you can indicate to whom you want each displayed. Also, the date on which you made the recommendation is displayed.

**Request a recommendation**

Whether you click the link to "Ask to be endorsed," or the tab "Request Recommendations," you are brought to the same LinkedIn screen.

It's really simple. Just complete a short form by selecting the position or school you want to be recommended for and then select the LinkedIn connections to send the request to. You can send a single request to up to 200 connections at one time.

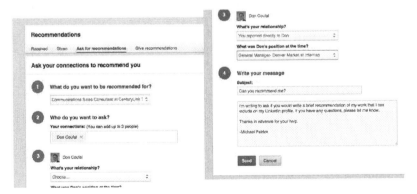

*Requesting LinkedIn Recommendations from others*

LinkedIn lets you pick which email address you would like the request to be sent from. We generally suggest the default, but make sure you choose one that actually works. (Remember we said NEVER delete an old email address from your LinkedIn database record!)

You have the option to customize the subject line and message text. We recommend keeping the default Subject text so that people recognize it easily. However, we highly recommend customizing the Message text to something more personable. Something like this:

> *"I'm getting more involved with LinkedIn now and I'm seeking recommendations for my past work. Would you mind writing me a recommendation for the sales engineering work I did at Random Access? Remember that project where we installed routers in 8 offices in one weekend and got it all done and working before workers showed up Monday morning? That was a great time wasn't it?*

> **Mike O'Neil**
> MyNewEmail@domain.com

It is important to note that you can only request recommendations from current 1st tier connections. Again, if you want to receive recommendations from others, it is better to send them a request via email with a link to your profile and instructions on how to submit a recommendation.

Tell them to start by clicking the link beside your picture or send them the instructions from our book! You can check the book Extras page for a quick link to a blog post describing the steps in detail.

## TIP

GET LinkedIn Recommendations by GIVING LinkedIn Recommendations. Yep, when you go first in recommending someone, LinkedIn has the nifty idea of asking them to "return the favor" and it's automatic!

# Chapter Nine

## Where Birds of a Feather
## Flock Together

# Linked**in**.
# Groups

LinkedIn Groups are where people of "similar interests" gather to share ideas. It's "Different Strokes for Different Folks" in many ways and there's something for just about everyone. Map out a plan for groups including which to join and how to manage it your group activity.

One of the most powerful features of LinkedIn is LinkedIn Groups. It has been around for a long time and there are hundreds of thousands of LinkedIn Groups bringing people with like interests together. LinkedIn has done a terrific job of adding value to Groups and continue to do so.

For example, fellow LinkedIn Group members are "in" each others' network. That is a huge feature, especially if you have this book! Fellow Group members are included in search results and you can typically send them a free message from within the LinkedIn group that you share with them. Now that's powerful!

Musical interests are well-represented in LinkedIn Groups. A quick LinkedIn Groups search on the keyword "Music" yields over 1,500 Groups, and "Band" yields another 300. There are four LinkedIn Groups about the Grateful Dead and three that focused on Led Zeppelin, for example.

*"Run with the pack"* (Bad Company, 1976)

While this is not the reason that we cover LinkedIn Groups in this book, it is a nice coincidence. Mike was at a recent Dead show (no longer the Grateful Dead) and there were lots of people with grey hair "tweeting" all around.

Groups are tightly tied to LinkedIn Profiles so we will cover it here. Lori reminds people in our classes that with LinkedIn groups you are putting your money where your mouth is. If you state in your interests section that you like Ford Mustangs like she does, then joining a group for Mustang Enthusiasts makes sense and also creates a statement of how important those "Interests" really are to you.

As a user, you can join up to 50 Groups (not including subgroups) and that should be plenty. We suggest that you identify 30 or so groups to join for starters and we will show you how to identify and join them.

**What are LinkedIn Groups?**

LinkedIn Groups are really a large number of independent gathering places on the LinkedIn site for people to come together over a topic that might be:

- A professional interest like Search Engine Optimization
- A professional association like the Business Marketing Association
- A region like Denver or Colorado
- A hobby like Corvettes or Horses
- A sport like Basketball or Tennis
- A fan club like Led Zeppelin or The Grateful Dead
- A cause like At Risk Children or Breast Cancer
- An alma mater like Arizona State University (Mike's)

# A LinkedIn Groups Plan

**LinkedIn Groups is so important that it really deserves to have its own plan, a plan within a plan, much like you did for LinkedIn Recommendations. We will touch on a number of ideas; some will strike you and others will not. We will clearly point out the MUST DO's.**

 **DETERMINE YOUR GOALS for LinkedIn Groups**

It will be different for everyone to a great degree; it might even be different for each user for each type of group. Here are some popular and noble goals:

To learn new ideas, best practices, event happenings and more from others in your line of business or in your region.

To meet others in your particular line of business, at your professional level or in your region.

To pose questions to an audience that can help you.

To get a nifty logo to post on your Profile. (This is the stamp that might confirm other statements in your profile. For example, if you say you are into Marketing, you should belong to some marketing related groups and show at least a couple of them on your profile.)

Note: when you join a group, you can adjust the settings including whether or not a particular group shows on your profile. This allows others to see the group, and, in addition to confirming your interest, helps promote the group.

 **DEVELOP A STRATEGY for identifying LinkedIn Groups to join**

Here is one to consider as a starting point. Pick at least three groups to join in each of these categories:

- ♦ Groups in your profession
- ♦ Groups in your region (usually city or state)
- ♦ Groups of personal interest (hobby)
- ♦ Groups that might contain prospects or customers
- ♦ Groups that might contain possible business partners
- ♦ Any alma mater that might have a group

Think about getting an invitation, perhaps from someone you do not know that references a LinkedIn Group you respect, one in your industry or simply one that lets you know that person shares a personal interest with you. Doesn't it make you more interested in that person? When we receive invitations like that, we at least look at their profile to see if there are other interesting aspects we can glean from their profile.

 **3**   **FIND the groups that will help you accomplish your goals**

There are two primary methods to find LinkedIn Groups. The first is by means of the Group Search function and the second is by clicking directly on the icon of LinkedIn Groups that you see on other people's profiles. (Remember the Group promotion we mentioned above?)

The Group search function makes it very easy to find groups of interest to you based on KEYWORDS. You can access LinkedIn Groups area from any page on LinkedIn. It is always on the navigation bar. Simply click on the Groups TAB and select Groups Directory. Now, look to left and notice the Search Groups area. For most people, just ignore the drop down options, it's the Keyword field that you are most interested in.

If you are familiar with the Keyword search function on LinkedIn (People button or Companies button) then this will be old hat for you. If not, we will provide a little search education for you here.

Long ago, in the time of Abraham Lincoln, a brilliant mathematician named George Boole created a mathematical methodology used in junior high classrooms to this day. It is based around the principle of "sets."

Let's try and compress an entire math class into just a few lines of text. Let's roll up your sleeves for a moment.

## Some Examples

Now that we have real examples, let's translate this into actually finding LinkedIn groups. Use this process to get going:

- ◆ From any page, hover over Interests TAB in the LinkedIn navigation and you will see "Groups" as an option in the drop down menu. Click it and you are on your way.
- ◆ In the Search Groups keyword field on the left, enter the phrase you might like to search. Do not pay any attention to the categories and languages options for now.

The results appear in descending order of largest to smallest membership size. They also display the Group Summary and logo. Note that the keyword search only searches the Name and short descriptions of the groups, not the full descriptions. If you OWN a group, that's even more important to take note of. You may want to adjust the settings and include more related keywords in the short description (the one that shows us in search results, not the longer one for the group profile).

 **JOIN Groups from the Group Search Screen**

When searching in the Group Search, this step is actually very easy. The "Join this group" text link appears in each search listing. You are one click away from REQUESTING to join the group.

Some groups will automatically approve you and others will require the group manager to approve you. If you are not approved or if it seems to take a long time to get approved (two to three weeks or more,) send a message to the group manager, or withdraw the request and find another more active group.

Here are some hot tips that come from Mike's book dedicated specifically to LinkedIn Groups. They are also included in the Integrated Alliances LinkedIn Groups training.

### Which Groups should I join?

In general, unless it is a group that particularly interests you, only join the top groups. Search results are listed in order of largest to smallest. If there are less than 500 members, think twice, unless there is a specific reason the group interests you. Join the top two or three from each of the categories listed earlier.

The group manager is identified when you request to join. Click on the link and invite the group manager to connect to you. Write a nice custom note. These are typically well-connected people so it is usually beneficial to connect with them as well. Again, we're not just saying this! We and our fans have actually had business opportunities arise because of this practice.

From a couple of areas, you can select the order of your LinkedIn groups. Often this only affects how YOU see the groups under Groups/Your Groups. But order them in a way that makes the most sense to you personally. Put the most strategic groups based on how frequently you will access them at the top.

You can also get to this from the Account and Settings section. The Settings link is at the top on every LinkedIn page. It is in the lower left corner of the Settings options. It is fairly obvious what to do if you spend just a few minutes there.

 **5** FIND AND JOIN LinkedIn Groups from other LinkedIn Profiles

During the course of your routine use of LinkedIn, you are going to look at lots of profiles. Just about every LinkedIn users is a member of at least SOME LinkedIn Groups. LinkedIn makes it incredibly easy for you to join groups when you see that others are members too. Right form their profile, you can see the groups you have in common (Already a member in green) and, if you're not already a member, click the blue "Join" link and become a member.

If you keyword search using the People button or the LinkedIn Advanced Search screen, you will find lots of interesting people that already belong to LinkedIn Groups: perhaps groups that would also be of interest to YOU? Here are some ideas for individuals you might want to locate:

♦ People in the same profession as you. They deal with many of the same issues meaning there is insider knowledge that can be shared.

♦ People, at your same level in the "org chart." C-levels might seek out other C-levels or directors other directors, for example. With the ever expanding list of C-titles, many with lesser know designations are seeking each other out to share and learn best practices.

♦ People that might constitute customers or business partners. This is where they are, and now you can mix and mingle with them where they spend their time – in LinkedIn Groups they care about.

♦ Simply click on the logo's you see at the bottom of a user's profiles. This will take you directly to the Join Group screen for that particular LinkedIn Group. So long as you are not already enrolled in 50 groups, you can request to join on the spot. It's just that easy.

♦ Open Groups: want to be involved in more than 50 Groups? LinkedIn now lets you follow and participate in Groups that are "open." That's an internal setting directed by each Group owner. But it essentially let's people who are not members participate on varying levels in the Group without actually being a member.

(An example of this is a group we run "Fans of Gitomer". Anyone on LinkedIn can submit comments and discussions for approval. We want to protect our members so we lock it down a bit but we find it valuable to allow others who may not be able to join to at least share insights.)

 **6**   **Look into joining LinkedIn SUBGROUPS**

LinkedIn has another interesting feature called Subgroups. Once you are a member of a LinkedIn Group, you can take it to the next level IN SOME GROUPS - those that have taken the plunge and established subgroups to their main group.

As this feature is adopted more and more by group managers, there will be increased time spent within these subgroups. The idea of a subgroup is much like a breakout session at a conference. A subgroup is also analogous to Special Interest Group within what might already be a Special Interest Group.

The larger groups are more likely to have subgroups in place. You can take a look at our Linked To Denver Group (_www.joinlinkedtodenver.com_) to see subgroups in action. An even better example is Linked:HR with 20 subgroups, run by our friend and LinkedIn Group Guru, Olivier Taupin.

You can join up to 50 subgroups and they DO NOT count against LinkedIn's limit of 50 main groups that a user may join. To some extent, that is like joining 100 LinkedIn groups, although subgroups will have a much smaller, tighter audience.

# Managing Your LinkedIn Group Activity

**With as many as 50 LinkedIn Groups, the chatter can drive you nuts without a little help! Here's how to adjust your "sanity settings."**

Getting involved with LinkedIn Groups greatly increases your circle of connections and can impact your influence. Members of the same "pack" can join in Group discussions and even send messages to one another, like fellow fan club members might do.

_"We belong"_ (Pat Benatar, 1984) to the same LinkedIn Group, it's quite possible we have other things in common too. Once you join relevant groups the fun really begins. LinkedIn Groups requires participation to derive the most impact but it is worth it. Groups can be a really FUN tool!

With many groups being "open", you can follow more without joining and participate in discussion (depending on how the manager has set permissions) for even more impact. It's a way to engage without throwing in your hat on a limited resource. After all, you can only join 50 groups!

LinkedIn Groups are all the rage for good reason. People are on LinkedIn to meet and interact with others with whom they can establish valuable business relationships. When those others are more highly qualified, or when they share common interests with you, it is even better.

LinkedIn Groups let you self-associate with others who have similar interests, and they provide tools for collaboration with fellow group members.

### Group Settings

Find the LinkedIn Group Settings from your Settings screen. At the top right of any LinkedIn page, click the tiny down arrow beside your name, select Settings. In the tabs on the bottom left, select "Groups, Companies, & Applications". This will present Groups, Companies, Applications, and related Privacy Controls to you in the box to the right of the tabs.

*Managing your LinkedIn Group settings*

## Group Invitation Filtering: "Turn on/off group invitations"

This allows you to indicate if you are interested in receiving Group Invitations. In today's environment, there are over a million groups, and more are being added each day. Now, that number may seem overwhelming, but if you search on a topic you are interested in and join the largest of the groups meeting your target, you should be in good shape.

LinkedIn Groups give you a sense of belonging, sort of like a fan club in the real world. People that attend the same concerts tend to have other things in common too, don't they? For example, Pink Floyd or Grateful Dead fans tend to get along well with one another.

A search of LinkedIn Groups for "Band OR Music" brings up over 10,000 results! The keywords "Grateful Dead" brings up over 10 groups. In a way, LinkedIn Groups is where you rub elbows with your peers, people you share fun interests with, and even Social Media Rock Stars.

Since you can join up to 50 LinkedIn Groups (and 50 subgroups as well), you should probably belong to at least 20-30 groups. We always try to keep a few available slots (we belong to about 45 at any one time) so we can join groups that we run across daily while traveling through the profiles of others.

While you can't order the way LinkedIn Groups appear on your profile, you can adjust their order when you look at the "Your Groups" screen. List the ones you own or manage, then your favorites on top. Why have it be a random order? If you don't particularly like the order, whose fault is it now that you know you have the power to arrange them the way you want? Keep in mind the order is only affected on your own Groups screen. The way other people see your list still shows up randomly.

To change settings for the groups you manage and for those to which you belong, you either need to go to the individual group, click "More..." and "Your Settings", or adjust the notifications from the Groups tab in your account Settings screen as we described above.

The options include Visibility Settings, Contact Settings, and Updates Settings (which now redirects you to your Account Settings). Again, these choices will be determined by how much communication you want to receive from each group.

## TIP

Adjust your "Group Digest Emails" to something other than Daily except for the groups you actually WANT to hear from each day (like groups you manage). Otherwise, this feature can become overwhelming and may discourage you from taking full advantage of everything LinkedIn Groups have to offer.

### Groups Order and Display

Here is where you can change the order your Groups display on your My Groups section, as well as how many and in what order they show up on your navigation menu. You can show from one to ten on the menu. There are links on the right of each Group name that gives you easy access to Manager and Member settings.

The Contact Settings allows you to select one of your alternate email addresses to receive communications from the Group, so if you have a personal interest group, but your main email is your work address, here is where you can have the messages for this group go to a personal email address instead.

Remember to check where your group messages go if you discontinue using a work or personal email. If you do not do this, a perpetual message "One or more of your email addresses have bounced" will appear across the top of your home page. Without access to reconfirm the email, you won't be able to get rid of the message without help from LinkedIn.

# Chapter Ten

## Adding a little "this and that" to your profile

LinkedIn profiles have standard sections and OPTIONAL sections that can be added. The list seems to be growing all the time - Patents, Publications, Causes, Volunteering, Courses and a lot more. Learn about how to re-order profile sections and entries within sections.

LinkedIn can only do so much and they know it. This cannot be said for many others in the space who draw the line for what to include without the opportunity to provide valid credentials. LinkedIn does it through adding LinkedIn Applications and Adding New Sections.

Keen to the eye of new people entering the LinkedIn world is support for new profile content, a feature called "Add Sections". As LinkedIn puts it, "Add sections to reflect achievements and experiences on your profile."

Explore this as LinkedIn is adding new capabilities as they trial and prove new topics to include. It is DEFINITELY worth taking advantage of and returning to often. Highlighting these achievements here emphasizes them in a way that means these important credentials won't get lost elsewhere.

**So what sections can you add?**

For example, you can add: Certifications, Courses, Honors and Awards, Languages, Organizations, Patents, Projects, Publications, Skills, Test Scores, and Volunteer Experience & Causes.

Let's explain these particular sections a bit to help you recognize why and when to use these cool featured sections.

Note that for each of these added sections, empty fields that are not required do not appear on your profile so people won't ask why something is missing.

Also, if you change your mind about any section, in addition to dragging it around by clicking on the title and moving it, you can remove it by clicking on the "x" on the right side of the title bar.

Also, when indicating dates, the months are not required unless they are important to you. If all you know is the years, that's fine.

**Certifications**

The only required field is Certification Name (250 characters), but it also allows fields for Certification Authority (250 characters), License Number (max of 80 characters), and Dates (or you can enter the start date and select "This certificate does not expire").

This is perfect for professionals whose certification is not dependent upon their position, but rather on their career.

## Courses

You would indicate the Name of Course (a required field) but you can also add the course number and the "Occupation" for which it applies.

If you have taken professional development coursework related to a specific position, this is a way to strengthen your credibility for each position by indicating the additional coursework required or taken to make you stronger.

Of course, if you have specific courses you took at a college or university you can also indicate the course number and educational institution instead of the position to show educational work that applies to your overall career at each location. For example, Lori lists her MBA level work with Liberty University. That educational experience is the annotated with "This education is associated with:" and then a hyperlink to the Courses section with the number of courses.

Note you get 255 characters for the Name of Course, but only 25 characters with spaces for the Course Number. Each course is associated with an existing position or educational experience already on your profile.

A Special Note for Fellow Trainers, Professors, Educators:

Are you a trainer? Consider adding the courses you train or teach to this special coursework section and attach it to your position! We do! Don't forget a call to action at the end of the position description to let people know the courses are listed and how to get them.

### Honors and Awards

This starts with the Title of the award; a required field with a 255 character limit, but don't go over, this fields just truncates if you're not concise! The Issuer also has a character limit of 255 but it's not a required field. Next select the occupation (or school) where this was awarded and the date.

You then have a description field to explain how and why this award was won. We recommend that you use this space to describe what makes this especially significant. For example, were you selected from among a certain number of candidates, is it a peer reviewed award, what kind of rigor or achievement caused you to be selected?

This is such a great improvement for the LinkedIn Profile because we finally have a place to not only crow a little, but to tell people why we deserve to do so! And LinkedIn recognizes the importance of being able to identify this that they allow 2,000 characters to do so. Use the space well. Be as descriptive yet as concise as possible to avoid boring your readers. Remember, your profile is ultimately about what credential you have that will serve THEIR needs!

## Languages

The Languages section allows you to list the language and Elementary, Limited Working, Professional Working, Full Professional, or Native or Bilingual Proficiency. Straightforward; right?

## Organizations

Again, a straightforward section that allows you something more than the Groups and Associations free text field. Here you can indicate life membership in say, Rotary International or Phi Delta Sigma (Lori's great honor society), etc.

Again, the Name is a required field but this also asks for positions held, indicate Occupation (or school), Time Period (start and stop or ongoing) and a description field. You can almost hear us say these fields (Name and Positions Held) are 255 characters each, a selection field for Occupation and 2,000 characters for the free form descriptive text field.

## Now for some strategy

Lori has included her position as State Education and Certification Director for the International Association of Administrative Professionals as a position on her profile. She has five recommendations shown for that position. Now that she has added this also as an organization, the position shows a link to the organization as well.

Likewise, with her schooling at Pfeiffer University where she was granted admission to the Phi Delta Sigma Academic Honor Society, the school position indicates "This education is associated with: 1 Organization" with a link to the new section as well as the recommendations.

This can be important because it will help you weave the pieces of your history together into a coherent tapestry for your readers. They might ask, "Why was that important?" Or "I wonder what lead Lori to seek this education, take that course, obtain this certification, etc." By using these newer sections of LinkedIn to weave the strings together, you have the opportunity to complete the picture.

## Projects

Since it is similar to Patents and to Publications sections and likely to be used more often, we'll cover Projects here.

Name: 255 characters, select the Occupation (experience or education) associated with this project; indicate other team members (or inventors in the case of patents, or writers in the case of publications); you can provide a project URL, the time period again, include months and or years and indicate if it is ongoing), and a 2,000 character limited description.

## Skills

You can list up to 50 skills.

Again are listed in the order that you enter them and include a short skill, which is instantly recommended as you type. It also allows you to identify your proficiency level and years of experience. If you leave either of those two fields blank, they just don't show.

Use care in how you connect your proficiency level with years of experience. For example, no one will believe you to be credible if you claim expertise with only one year of experience. It's not a bad idea to either err on the side of caution, or just don't list either the years and/or the proficiency level. You don't want to be put into a position of justifying your answer or, worse of having people click the back button without ever telling you!

## Test Scores

This seems straight forward right? List the test, the date and the score. It could be SAT or ACT, it could be certification exams. In addition to the required Name, Score and Date field, you can once again select the Occupation and a 2,000 character description.

## Volunteer Experience & Causes

You know that we've recommended for years to add Volunteer Experience with your paid positions. Now LinkedIn allows you to let them stand apart. That's powerful for so many reasons, not the least of which is for those who volunteer concurrently with other positions and don't want the volunteer position to appear above their primary paid employment. By using Add Sections, you can differentiate this experience while maintaining your current professional focus.

Even if you don't have experience, but are interested in causes, you can select from a list of "What causes you care about" and you can indicate "Which organizations you support" (if they have a company profile on LinkedIn!).

For the Causes you support, you can select from the listing. If you select "Other" it allows you to free type text (for example, Music Education) and click the "Add another cause" up to 5 additional causes.

For the Organizations you support, type in their name and, if they are on LinkedIn (organization or company page, it will show the matching organization in a drop down list. If not, you will be able to enter free form text.

You can also complete an additional form that allows you to enter free form text to name the organization, your role the time period and a 2,000 maximum character description. It also allows you to indicate the related type of cause (such as Animal Welfare, Arts and Culture, Children, etc.)

This is a rockin' way to personalize your profile. People are passionate about causes. If you need a tie-breaker with who will do business with you, let it be a shared passion like causes. But use care... some causes are not as appropriate to talk about in a public business environment.

# Moving Sections Where You Want Them

Wouldn't it be great to simply move sections of your LinkedIn Profile around like you move furniture around your home?

The major sections (i.e., Summary) have a little pointed grab bar you can use to drag and drop entire sections. It has some drawbacks though.

There are some important issues to note. First, people are used to seeing things in a certain order; at least that is true for more established LinkedIn users, so changes that go too far can have people quickly clicking the "Back" button.

While you can move entire LinkedIn Profile sections around, you cannot move information within some sections (like ordering applications). Applications appear in the reverse order of installation.

Some records are meant to be played as laid down, especially on vinyl. The songs are in that order for a reason and we don't just mean rock operas like _"Tommy: Pinball Wizard"_ (The Who with Elton John, 1980)!

But in our case, with so many Recommendations, viewers had to scroll through 60 pages to see Additional Information Section (Interests, Groups, etc.) and Contact Settings at the bottom. To Mike, moving Recommendations to the Bottom seems like a good idea.

But most people also know that Contact Settings are typically near the bottom, so Lori moved Additional Information above Recommendations and left Contact Settings at the very end. (A quick tip to move to the bottom of a webpage is to press Ctrl+End. You can quickly get back to the top with Ctrl+Home.)

We've seen people who had a few good strong recommendations put those just after the summary because they felt the recommendations were more important than their "resume".

People often are ready to reach out to us and they want to go to our profile, quickly get a phone number or email address, and make that live connection. Therefore, it seems to make sense to put Personal Information or Contact Settings near the top. So Lori moved her Personal Information to the top. Mike has both Personal Information and Contact Settings near the top of his Profile.

You might take a look at our profiles to see how the sections are arranged now. Remember that we are always experimenting! Be sure to consider your options and choose the best order to help you convey credibility and trust to your prospects. What is the best flow for your information?

And, finally, just because you can move sections, this might not be one to move. Since it appears at the bottom of most profiles, that's where people will expect to find it. Mike moved his up just below his Summary and Specialties because his profile is so long. Lori kept hers at the bottom. For most, we recommend leaving it at the bottom so it will be where people expect to find it. Don't make them work too hard to learn how to reach out.

# Appendix

## A la carte

Material that is "off the beaten path" is here including getting started from scratch. See a head to head Facebook and LinkedIn comparison. Taking LinkedIn to the limit shows you how far to go. The LinkedIn glossary explains the jargon. The author's and their unique relationship with LinkedIn Corp. is explained. Read about the RockTheWorld with LinkedIn Radio show, enjoy the Book's Soundtrack Set List in one consolidated listing.

# A True LinkedIn Virgin?

**If you're not yet a LinkedIn user, now's the time. Don't use LinkedIn's quick start utility, use this book instead and save LOTS of editing!!**

You can't get started in the LinkedIn world until you have a LinkedIn Profile. While LinkedIn makes getting started very easy, getting a Rockstar LinkedIn Profile takes time and/or some help.

You may be tempted to use some of the slick tools that LinkedIn provides to shorten the process (like uploading your resume), but this book does an infinitely better job than a "resume-parsing" tool.

After all, LinkedIn Profiles are NOT resumes; they are a dynamic representation of you as a professional interested in taking your success to the next level.

If you already have a LinkedIn presence, you can pick up the needle and move it to the next song on the record, or simply read along. There is much to be said about hearing the WHOLE RECORD isn't there?

So, _"You Wanna' Be Starting Something"_ (Michael Jackson, 1984) and creating your LinkedIn account is where it starts. Creating a "stub" of a profile is the very first step in creating an account. LinkedIn prompts you with a few questions and creates it for you.

It is really quite easy to sign up on LinkedIn. You simply type _www.LinkedIn.com_ into your browser. There are simple instructions for both new and returning users.

Newbies will need to sign up by entering some basic information like First and Last Name, email Address, Password, etc. It only takes about five minutes to complete these initial steps. Once you have your account, it's time to get going!.

Do not select the options to import a resume or to automatically find and invite any people. It is tempting but you will soon know better why not to take this approach.

## Some Handy Menu Definitions

**TAB** – LinkedIn has TABs called Home, Profile, Contacts, Groups, Jobs, Inbox, Companies and More.

**Menu Items** – The options that appear upon hovering over a TAB. You move your mouse down and click on the Menu Item.

**Sub-Menu Items** – The options that appear upon hovering over a TAB.

## TIP

If you should find you have more than one LinkedIn profile you have a problem. It's not allowed and it's confusing. Search on your own name and see if this might be you.

# LinkedIn vs. Facebook, A Comparison

**It helps to have something to compare LinkedIn to and Facebook is the obvious choice; or is it really the other way around? Hmmm......**

Analogies between LinkedIn and Facebook weren't very useful when we started training on LinkedIn. In fact, only students could even get on Facebook back then. Nowadays, however, it is useful to compare and contrast them.

*How LinkedIn and Facebook stack up, head to head*

LinkedIn and Facebook will continue to be directly compared for a long time. Perhaps it's the IPO's that will bring them into more comparisons.

Facebook is a better comparison than Twitter. Both have personal profiles, business pages and capped 2-way networks. They're more alike than different.

We say this a lot in our live trainings – LinkedIn is EASY, Social Media is HARD. Preparing fresh corn on the cob is far less complex than preparing a cob salad.

With this book to get you started, LinkedIn is a yellow brick road that can take you to Oz. LinkedIn is like a big sturdy ship. It doesn't move quickly but it has a major payload.

Facebook, on the other hand, is a *"Land of Confusion"* (Genesis, 1984), more like *"Goodbye Yellow Brick Road"* (Elton John, 1974). It is more of a moving target, like a speedboat, and it will probably always be that way.

While there are similar *categories*, there are major DIFFERENCES between LinkedIn and Facebook.

|  | **LinkedIn** | **Facebook** |
|---|---|---|
|  |  |  |
| **Real Life Mirror** | Business Commerce | The College Experience |
| **Profile** | Fully Searchable | NOT Easily Searchable |
| **Network Size** | 30,000 Connections | 5,000 Friends |
| **Network Type** | Three Levels Deep | Single Level |
| **Pictures** | One, Headshot | Extensive, Galleries, Video |
| **Applications** | No Longer | Almost a Million |
| **Web Sites** | 3 | Many |
| **Endorsements** | Recommendations | None |

LinkedIn and Facebook ask for some of the SAME information.

|  | **LinkedIn** | **Facebook** |
|---|---|---|
|  |  |  |
| **Jobs** | Experience | Employers |
| **School** | Education | College, High School |
| **Personal:** | Interests | Sports |
|  | Interests | Arts & Entertainment |
|  | Interests | Activities & Interests |
|  | Summary, Specialties | Basic Information |
|  | Personal Information | Contact Information |

### Differences

LinkedIn and Facebook also have a number of entirely different pieces of information they prompt for and track.

Areas where Facebook has no direct match to LinkedIn include:

Sex (male/female), Anniversary, Relationship Status, Music, Books, Movies, Television, Political Views, People that Inspire You, Favorite Quotes, Sports You Play, Favorite Athletes, Favorite Teams.

LinkedIn, to its credit, has a FEW unique profile areas, namely Groups and Associations, Honors and Awards and Recommendations. They all seem pretty businesslike don't they? They are!

# Taking LinkedIn to the Limit

**Most things in the social media world have limits and LinkedIn is no different. It's really important to know your limits.**

"I only have 3,000 invitations; only 300 characters to invite someone to join your network? I didn't know that!"

With few exceptions, everything within LinkedIn has limits. After all, it is a database! Being curious and used to getting the maximum benefit we could, we set out to find the limits on LinkedIn. LinkedIn's limits, like the 3,000 Invitation limit or the 50 Group limit, really matter and you MUST plan accordingly or you can be stuck in the desert with no food or water.

In some cases it is really important to know about the limits. Some of them have irreversible consequences, e.g. having 3,000 invitations or only listing 25 skills. At the same time there are areas without limits, e.g. the number of experiences or schools or email accounts. For example, the Summary section has 2,000 characters; how many should you use? Prince has the answer: "1999" of course!

Think of different ways to express yourself and your message to your target audience then effectively use the space LinkedIn affords you. Fill it up, "_Take it to the limit_" (The Eagles, 1975) .

## The LinkedIn Counter

In many cases, LinkedIn will be really helpful and tell you when you go _"One toke over the line"_ (Brewer and Shipley, 1970) by counting the characters for you and letting you know what the max is so you know how much you need to trim. It is even turns red when you cross "0" so you really can't miss it. This counter tool is showing up more and more and it's a great development.

For example, if you paste text into your summary text box, click on "Save" and you're over, it will tell you that have used, for example, 2,050 characters and you are only allowed 2,000. It won't let you save it until you comply with the limits. (Note that on the Contact Settings free form text field, it doesn't do this yet. Rather it goes back to your profile without saving what you entered... another reason to write it in Word first then copy/paste!)

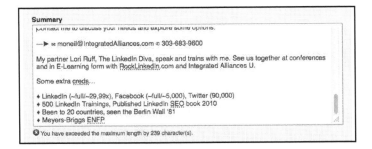

*LinkedIn helps you when you go over the limit with RED text*

You can almost tell what the limits of many fields will be based on the type of field it is. For example, the free form text fields named "Description" no matter where you find it, is 2,000 characters. The fields with titles, company names, and education are all 100. Most fields that are the name of something (i.e., Certification Name, Certification Authority, Organization Name, etc) are 250 while others are 255. Additional sections that might mirror descriptions (such as Interests and Groups and Associations) are 1,000.

The following identifies the maximum # of characters allowed in most fields.

## LinkedIn Profile Limits

**Number of Profiles**          Legally 1, technically there is no limit

## Picture

At 4 MB, you will seldom find the file you upload is too large for LinkedIn. Upload your photo, crop it a little if you need to and save it. Be sure to start with a file at least 450 x 450 pixels since that is the "native size" for LinkedIn. This way, visitors can click on your picture and enlarge it to a full 450 x 450 pixels.

## Major Profile Sections

| | |
|---|---|
| **First Name** | 20 characters |
| **Last Name** | 40 characters |
| **Former/Maiden Name** | 40 characters |
| **Headline** | 120 characters |
| **Website Custom Tag** | 30 characters |
| **Status field** | 140 characters if you want it all to show on Twitter, otherwise 600 characters |
| **Public Profile URL** | 30 characters |
| **Summary** | 2,000 characters |
| **Number of Experiences** | unlimited |

*A la carte*

| | |
|---|---|
| **Company Name** | 100 characters |
| **Company Display Name** | 100 characters |
| **Position (Job) Title** | 100 characters |
| **Position Description** | 2,000 characters |

## Number of Educational Institutions - unlimited

| | |
|---|---|
| **Degree** | 100 characters |
| **Field of Study** | 100 characters |
| **Activities and Societies** | 500 characters (hyperlinked field needing comma/space) |
| **Additional Notes** | 1,000 characters |
| **# of Recommendations** | unlimited |
| **Recommendation Text** | more than you should ever use! |
| **Interests** | 1,000 characters (hyperlinked field needing comma/space) |
| **Groups and Associations** | 1,000 characters (hyperlinked field needing comma/space) |
| **Honors and Awards** | 1,000 characters |
| **Contact Settings** | 2,000 characters |

## Additional Sections

| | |
|---|---|
| **Courses** | 50 characters |
| **Name of Course** | 255 characters |
| **Course Number** | 25 characters |

## Certifications

| | |
|---|---|
| **Certification Name** | 250 characters (required) |
| **Certification Authority** | 250 characters |
| **License Number** | 80 characters |

## Honors and Awards

| | |
|---|---|
| **Title of the award** | 255 characters (required) |
| **Issuer** | 255 characters |
| **Description** | 2,000 characters |

## Languages

| | |
|---|---|
| **Language** | 80 characters |
| **Proficiency** | Select from list |

## Organizations

| | |
|---|---|
| **Name** | 255 characters (required) |
| **Position Held** | 255 characters |
| **Description** | 2,000 characters |

## Patents, Projects & Publications

| | |
|---|---|
| **Title** | 255 characters |
| **Publication/Publisher** | 255 characters |
| **Patent/Application Number** | 60 characters |

Other Contributors (Team Members for Projects, Inventors for patents, Authors for publications) – 10 total with 110 characters for their name

## Skills

| | |
|---|---|
| **Number Allowed** | 50 characters |
| **Length** | 50 characters |

## Test Scores

| | |
|---|---|
| **Name** | 255 characters |
| **Score** | 20 characters |
| **Description** | 2,000 characters |

## Volunteer Experience & Causes

| | |
|---|---|
| **Causes you support** | there are only a limited number available to select from, including Other, which lets you add up to 5 more causes with 100 characters per field to describe it |
| **Organizations you support** | unlimited |
| **Volunteer Experiences** | unlimited |

## Other Important LinkedIn Limits (for all users)

| | |
|---|---|
| **Total Number of Direct Tier 1 Connections** | 30,000 |
| **Invitations you can send to others** | 3,000* |

\* If you run out, you can request up to 500 more from LinkedIn customer service every 30 days. You must be at 0 or near it before they will typically grant your request.

| | |
|---|---|
| **Invitations you can accept** | 30,000 |
| **Number of people you can send a message to at once** | 50 |

\*You may only send to Tier 1 connections

| | |
|---|---|
| **Number of LinkedIn Groups you may join** | 50* |

\*Plus 50 more subgroups)

| | |
|---|---|
| **# Status updates per day** | no limit* |

\* be careful not to "go overboard"

## On a final note…

Where you see "Edit" in the Section header, you will typically be limited in how many you can list. List is the important word here. It is a list of, for example, your Skills or Languages or Courses. We have found no limits of "how many you can list," for example with Experiences, Projects and Publications. In these Section headers, there is only "Add…" and no "Edit." Here's a screen shot to show you what we mean.

*LinkedIn lets you enter Projects, Publications, Patents and more*

# LinkedIn Glossary

It is easy to throw words around and think that everyone knows what you mean. What does "contact" stand for? How about "connection"? When you define the terms, you get everyone on the same page. You always know where John Mellencamp stands on things. He is the very definition of Rock & Roll - no filler, no substitute, nothing artificial. He is rock in its purest, most definitive sense.

**Companies**: On LinkedIn, Companies can have a Company Page (a topic for another book!) that highlights their company description, specialties, employees, location and "public" information, and career opportunities. The Company page admin has access to simple analytics. Company pages can have followers and host a Twitter stream to provide more current and relevant information to viewers and/or to followers through the Network Updates to their home pages.

**Connection:** Someone with whom you are directly connected on LinkedIn. Sometimes you will see the word Direct or Tier 1 used or someone may be described as being a "1." These phrases all mean the same thing.

You have special capabilities with your Tier 1 connections. Beside the name of each person who is a peer, you will see "1st" beside their name indicating their relationship to you. Their first level connections, with whom you are not connected, will display "2nd", and the connections of your Tier 2 connections will display "3rd". Finally, LinkedIn indicates people with whom you share a group as "Group". These are treated in sort results the same as Tier 2s.

**Contact:** Someone whose contact information has been imported into your LinkedIn space, but is not yet connected to you (these are like prospects.)

**Groups:** LinkedIn Groups are akin to virtual networking events where the group members have like interests. These groups can be focused on a geographic area, a common business industry or interest, or a personal interest. This is a popular feature of LinkedIn that enhances a member's ability to network effectively to achieve their goals.

**Inbox:** this is LinkedIn's messaging area. By default, most messages that arrive in your LinkedIn Inbox also are forwarded to your regular email. However, those settings can be adjusted to moderate the influx to your regular email client. Even if you answer the messages by regular email, you must still clear the messages from your LinkedIn inbox. From you LinkedIn Inbox, you can reply, forward, archive, delete, star, or report a message as spam. Types of messages include invitations, introductions, requests for recommendations, messages from group members, etc.

**InMail:** An inner-platform email message that is sent through the system usually to second or third level connections. It replaces the Introduction process. It is NOT used or needed between direct Tier 1 connections. A certain number of InMails are granted monthly to paid subscribers based on their level of service. Free members can also purchase InMails for $10 each.

LinkedIn now also allows "partner InMails" which are sent to LinkedIn members via targeted messages from a partner who pays LinkedIn to send these messages. These are not sent to a specific person who they can see, as with paid members described above, but are sent based on anonymous demographic targets that the advertiser provides LinkedIn. LinkedIn then matches those targets with members to decide who to send the InMails (or Paid Messages) to.

**Introduction:** A request for a message along with your contact information passed through one individual to another for a business introduction. There are two levels of introduction, through one person to get to a 2nd level connection, or through two to get to a 3rd level connection. This is sort of like passing notes in class ... not a recommendation or endorsement. It is best not to use this for Tier 3 connections as the introduction can often be delayed, causing you to run out of available introductions.

**Invitation:** Asking someone to "join your professional network on LinkedIn." The end result is that each becomes a part of the other's network of LinkedIn contacts, giving both the ability to search through more records to find opportunities. It doesn't matter who invites whom, the result is being connected just as if one person picked up the phone to call the other and got an answer.

**Jobs:** On LinkedIn, Jobs is an area that allows you to search for job postings by recruiters, HR, and hiring managers. A nifty feature is "People Who Viewed This Job Also Viewed…"

**Network:** The people to whom you are directly connected on LinkedIn, their direct connections and their direct connections – three levels deep. It also includes people with whom you share a group – these are treated as Tier 2 connections when sorting search results by "Relationship."

**Network Updates:** On your LinkedIn homepage, by default, you see the updates of people you are connected to, companies you are following and groups of which you are a member. This is a great place to get a quick overview of what your connections are up to. It allows you to quickly like, comment, share or send a message to the person who posted. Additional items that show up here are when your connections post in groups, follow a company or update their profile (as long as the default settings are left on).

**News:** news is now shown on your LinkedIn homepage just under your status update field under "LinkedIn Today." These are popular headlines shared by your connections. In addition, LinkedIn's navigation bar includes a News tab that gives you quick access to LinkedIn Today (the equivalent of a personalized online newspaper populated with articles shared by your connections), articles you have saved, and Signal, a feature that allows you to monitor and search the Twitter conversations of your LinkedIn network.

**OpenLink:** These messages are when a paid subscriber indicates their willingness to accept InMail from anyone. Users can send OpenLink members a free InMail. When paid subscribers send an OpenLink message, it is not counted against their available InMails.

**Organizations:** Similar to Companies, Organizations are available to include in your LinkedIn Profile along with causes you support, volunteer positions you have held, and memberships you want to highlight. Each of these adds credibility to your professional history.

**Profile:** Your personal identity on LinkedIn; your data record in LinkedIn's database. It is the equivalent of a professional Web page about you with special links and other features that allow you to impact your business.

According to LinkedIn's EULA (End User License Agreement), there is only one profile per person. Each profile is to be used by an individual—not a company—and there is to be NOTHING in your Name fields other than your real name and any lettered credentials or you risk LinkedIn shutting down your account.

**Search:** Looking for people, companies, or groups on LinkedIn based on specific information. It may be a name, a location, a keyword, or other search criteria. Combine the power of the search three levels deep and reach into Group relationships with many options to find specific or targeted results.

This is the most powerful feature of LinkedIn. A really well built-out and SEO-friendly profile will make your LinkedIn Profile more searchable and, therefore, more findable. (By the way, SEO stands for Search Engine Optimization.)

**Search Engine Optimization (SEO):** Computer programs ("bots") constantly look through the Internet, LinkedIn and other platforms to find information based on a user's search criteria. It is based on words and/or phrases.

In the LinkedIn world, people can find your LinkedIn Profile through its internal search function. Better yet, LinkedIn Profiles are "fully indexed" or searchable by Google and most other search engines as well, making your presence on LinkedIn, and a well-built profile, even more important.

Although your LinkedIn Profile is "fully indexed," the indexing process does not include your Personal Information Section, Contact Settings Section and other sensitive fields.

**Tier:** A Tier indicates relationship level. It defines how many people are between you and someone else in terms of relationships. Another way to think of this is that a Tier 1 connection is directly connected to you; a Tier 2 connection is someone connected to them. There are three Tiers in LinkedIn. Group members are like friends with whom you share a common interest.

**Want to know more? email Training@IntegratedAlliances.com with your question. We'll answer to you both privately and on our blog.**

# LinkedIn Corp. and The LinkedIn Rockstars

**While LinkedIn sponsored our first LinkedIn hands-on workshop trainings, we have no formal relationship with LinkedIn or any of the other Social Media providers.**

We must be very clear in stating that we are not associated with LinkedIn (or any other social media platform mentioned) in any way. We are constantly asked this question as we have provided much support to the LinkedIn user community for many years. It is simply not the case.

We are more like at-will evangelists for LinkedIn and the greater social media community. There are more and more people like us all the time, people who really "get LinkedIn." They usually reach out to us as established leaders with some of the largest LinkedIn networks in the world. We have actually trained hundreds of these insightful individuals that now train on LinkedIn and social media themselves and provide services.

If there were a better tool to accomplish professional success rather than LinkedIn, we'd be all over it. The fact is, there isn't a better tool at this time. We work for YOU, the user community, rather than LinkedIn.

The same statement goes for Twitter, Facebook and all of the other social media platforms. We simply do not have formal relationships any more than other users may have. We are paid LinkedIn subscribers, we operate LinkedIn Groups, we do some pay per click on the platforms.

As a business, we are a traditional "for profit" company that gives back, a LOT. We operate in a manner much like other associations, user groups, and fan clubs. We anticipate the needs of the LinkedIn and social media user community and we respond to serve those needs. We host monthly Meetups to educate the community on WordPress, LinkedIn, Facebook, Twitter and all of social media – free training events in Colorado.

That said we wish to thank LinkedIn for many things:

First, we wish to thank LinkedIn for creating this incredible platform in the first place. It caters so well to our own internal needs, and to the business we have built around it. Because of the power and influence of LinkedIn today, this industry has a strong business focus.

Thousands of people have their jobs today because of LinkedIn, and we don't just mean jobs at LinkedIn. An entire industry has sprung up in which we play a major role. This industry employs thousands more, perhaps tens of thousands. These are business professionals who would have never pictured themselves in such an exciting role or working for such an interesting company as they do now.

Second, we want to thank LinkedIn Corp. for their sponsorship of our early LinkedIn Hands-on Workshops way back in early 2006. LinkedIn was generous to help us launch the formal LinkedIn training programs from the ground level with some financial backing.

Third, for their continued product development and enhancements that provide business users with increased functionality, which allow companies to find customers, partners, and employees, and enable displaced individuals to find needed employment. The lives of most users are better as a result.

Special thanks go directly to Reed Hoffman for the help he provided to our strategic business partner, The Rockies Venture Club, by keynoting the 2006 RVC Colorado Capital Conference. His appearance helped cement LinkedIn as the quintessential online business capital player in Colorado that it is today..

Thanks LinkedIn!

*Mike O'Neil with LinkedIn Executive Chairman and Co-Founder Reid Hoffman at the Colorado Capital Conference in 2006.*

# About The LinkedIn Rockstars

**We love to connect up with our fans, to become friends with our fans, so please reach out to us.**

We really enjoyed putting this book together to help you be more successful on LinkedIn and in your business. Mike likes putting in his extras touches, spicing things up with Classic Rock and technology and Lori enjoys sharing career-oriented content and getting to the nitty-gritty detail of HOW to do things.

As super-connected individuals and perhaps the most connected LinkedIn couple on the planet, we experience LinkedIn and social media from a little different perspective than most. We find that this is useful for helping you and it arms us with terrific material to speak and train on these topics. We hope to meet you when we are out on tour. Bring the book and we will be happy to sign it and even take pictures if you like!

To who like to cut to the chase, and for those with short attention spans like Mike, we offer a free LinkedIn Profile InfoGuide at _LinkedeBook.com_ that summarized this book in just 4 pages.

Mike O'Neil is an entrepreneur, an expert LinkedIn trainer and a former IT professional and sales engineer. In 2003, Mike founded Integrated Alliances (IA) as a professional business networking organization presenting business networking events, first in Colorado and now nationwide for providing the most effective business development gatherings for professionals who want to uncover business opportunities.

Mike expanded the role of Integrated Alliances in early 2006 as online networking gained in popularity. IA began training business professionals to use LinkedIn focused on business applications, and now IA has trained thousands of people in hundreds of sessions, including hands-on workshops and conferences across North America and in online webinars with a world-wide reach. Mike became a LinkedIn user in January 2004 – user number 125,841.

Headquartered in Denver, CO, Mike has assembled a team of social media professionals represented in metropolitan areas coast to coast. Most of them he met or reconnected with through LinkedIn and other social media platforms. They typically have reached out to Mike to join his team of dynamic social media trainers and coaches and to become associated with the brand that is IA. In addition, IA has courted collaborative partnerships with some of the biggest names in this exploding industry.

Lori Ruff joined the national expansion team in Charlotte, NC mid-2008 after meeting Mike on LinkedIn of all places! Later that year, she was asked to join the IA executive team, and did so with fervor. While Mike provides much of the vision, Lori is remarkable at making sure the right ideas are implemented at the right time. It is truly a brilliant partnership.

Her current career began in July 1996, when she founded a training and consulting firm winning government contracts, corporate clients, and multiple awards. Lori joined the LinkedIn community in July 2005 when Facebook was still in school. She has long been known as a connector of people and now uses social networking to enhance those skills. She has become a respected authority in the world of social media and LinkedIn training.

Today Lori is a popular speaker, trainer, and online business reputation consultant delivering with poise and high energy. She has presented more than 1,800 hours representing almost 800 training sessions and seminar appearances to audiences as large as 500. She is also a Microsoft Certified Master Instructor and speaks on topics such as customer service, leadership, visioning, personal development, and career transition.

# RockTheWorld with LinkedIn Radio Show

Mike O'Neil, Lori Ruff and other members of the Integrated Alliances LinkedIn Rockstar team host the RockTheWorld with LinkedIn Radio show each week on *WebmasterRadio.FM*.

They interview a variety of guests:

- ♦ CEO's of and technologists from social media service providers
- ♦ LinkedIn and social media experts from around the world
- ♦ Industry visionaries that know where the world is headed
- ♦ Musicians that utilize social media effectively

Some examples of guests include Nimble CEO Jon Ferrara, Pure Matter CEO Bryan Kramer, Vorsight CEO Steve Richard, AA-ISP Founder Larry Reeves, landing page expert Tim Ash, visionary Stan Slap, International social media expert Sundeep Kapur, Social Media expert Mark Schaefer, Twitter expert Joel Comm, social media expert Mark Fidelman and HUNDREDS of others.

These 30-minute shows are interesting for a variety of reasons. Some shows are mostly about technology, some are more about how the companies were formed, some are about the future. Most shows have at least a little conversation about music, concerts and the like (and some have a lot). Audiences get to really know the guest at a personal level.

Most shows finish with "expert segments" that are packed with 5 minutes of hard-hitting tips from experts.

WebmasterRadio.FM show producer Jorge "Brasco" Hermida is a world-class podcasting expert and he makes the show look and sound excellent while he infuses rock music into each show.

Learn more about the company behind the show and see if sponsorship might be a good idea for you at *www.WebmasterRadio.FM.*

Listen to past episodes at *www.RockstarNetworking.com.*

# Soundtrack Set List

**Mike did most of the music integration for the book. It's just the way he is hooked on the inspiration of rock music.**

Most of the music in this book is part of Mike's personal library. Here are the songs in the book in chronological order:

*"A Day in the Life"* (The Beatles, 1967)

*"All I want to do"* (Sheryl Crow, 1994)

*"Are you experienced?"* (Jimi Hendrix, 1967)

*"Both Sides Now"* (Joni Mitchell, 2000)

*"Call me"* (Blondie, 1980)

*"Changes"* (David Bowie, 1974)

*"Don't stop"* (Fleetwood Mac, 1977)

*"Fame"* (David Bowie, 1975)

*"Free Bird"* (Lynyrd Skynyrd, 1975)

*"Goodbye Yellow Brick Road"* (Elton John, 1974)

*"Heard it through the grapevine"* (Marvin Gaye, 1968)

*"Helter Skelter"* (The Beatles, 1966)

*"I can't go for that"* (Hall and Oates, 1981)

*"I feel like a number"* (Bob Seger, 1981)

*"I get by with a little help from my friends"* (The Beatles, 1967)

*"I Know a Little"* (Lynyrd Skynyrd, 1974)

*"Land of Confusion"* (Genesis, 1984)

*"Like to get to know you well"* (Howard Jones, 1984)

*"Livin' in the past"* (Jethro Tull, 1972)

*"Man in the mirror"* (Michael Jackson, 1988)

*"Message in a bottle"* (The Police, 1979)

*"My Hometown"* (Bruce Springsteen, 1989)

*"My Old School"* (Steely Dan, 1973)

*"No Lookin' Back"* (Michael McDonald, 1985)

*"Old Days"* (Chicago, 1975)

*"One toke over the line"* (Brewer and Shipley, 1970)

*"Photograph"* (Def Leppard, 1983)

*"Run with the pack"* (Bad Company, 1976)

*"Same Old Song and Dance"* (Aerosmith 1974)

*"School's out"* (Alice Cooper, 1972)

*"See me, feel me"* (The Who, 1970)

*"Shout it Out Loud"* (KISS, 1977)

*"Show Me the Way"* (Peter Frampton, 1973)

*"Start Me Up"* (The Rolling Stones 1981)

*"Stayin' alive"* (The Bee Gees, 1977)

*"Still Crazy After All These Years"* (Paul Simon, 1977)

*"Suite Judy Blue Eyes"* (Crosby, Stills and Nash, 1976)

*"Take it to the limit"* (The Eagles, 1975)

*"Taking Care of Business"* (Bachman Turner Overdrive, 1976)

*"The Heart of the Matter"* (Don Henley, 1989)

*"The real me"* (The Who, 1973)

*"Tommy: Pinball Wizard"* (The Who with Elton John, 1980)

*"True colors"* (Cyndi Lauper, 1986)

*"Two out of three ain't bad"* (Meatloaf, 1977)

*"Walk this way"* (Aerosmith, 1975)

*"We belong"* (Pat Benatar, 1984)

*"Welcome to the machine"* (Pink Floyd, 1975)

*"What you need"* (INXS, 1985)

*"What's goin' on"* (Marvin Gaye, 1971)

*"Who Are You?"* (The Who, 1973)

*"You Wanna' Be Starting Something"* (Michael Jackson, 1984)

*"You've got a friend"* (James Taylor, 1971)

## Rock Note

"It's the end of the world as we know it and I feel fine..."

The now separated band REM was offered big money ($ millions) by Microsoft to use this song in the Marketing of Windows 95. The band balked and Microsoft instead selected *"Start Me Up"* (The Rolling Stones 1981).

So, did the Song come before the START Button or was START always the name of the now famous button? Hmmm...

# Classic Rock Is Timeless, So Is This Book!

**Online additions to "RockTheWorld" give it a really long shelf life, like a timeless rock song that is remade, covered and even "sampled" to make it new again.**

Rock & Roll is timeless and this book is relatively timeless as well. While no "how-to" technology book can keep from growing obsolete, we have taken major steps to keep the material current and relevant. Unlike a brand new car that loses its value the moment you drive it off the lot, your investment in this or any "RockTheWorld™" book is safe.

The finer details of LinkedIn Profile development and MUCH MORE are always kept up to date online at _www.RockTheWorldBook.com_. When you arrive, you will find current blogs and tutorials, screen shots, videos, and lots of helpful and really FUN things to help you build on the momentum you started with your spiffin' LinkedIn Profile!

_"Both Sides Now"_ (Joni Mitchell, 2000) puts the spotlight on the book side and the online side that have become commonplace in this world of Kindle, iPad, obsolete print editions and the like.

It is a double-edged sword. You want the book to include all the instructions so it is all right there, self-contained. On the flip side, it can change so that the content isn't correct anymore. This is our attempt at drawing the line at the right point. Please share your feedback at Training@IntegratedAlliances.com

While you are at the site, you can take in the other material we have for you as well. With few exceptions it is all free. The site includes a wide array of information on LinkedIn and the greater spectrum of social media.

Our online site continues the Rock & Roll attitude of the book and even takes it to a whole new dimension. Visit often as it is never the _"Same Old Song and Dance"_ _(Aerosmith 1974)_ . It rocks just like the Aerosmith album "Rocks" does!

## Special Thanks

Our dear friend Judith Briles, known as The Book Shepherd (_www.TheBookShepherd.com_) has been our trusted advisor on this book and other book projects and we want to thank her here.

Judith runs Author U (_www.AuthorU.ORG_) and she hosts the big **Author U Extravaganza** event every May in Denver, Colorado.

If you're considering a book project or have book-related questions, we suggest you reach out to her.

# Buying Books

**RockTheWorld with LinkedIn v2.1** is available in print or eBook form for Kindle, Apple and other popular formats. This book replaces v1.0 and v2.0.

## Individual Orders

For individual books or "small orders, the book can be purchased at *www.RockTheWorldBook.com* or directly on Amazon.com.

## Large Orders

RockTheWorld with LinkedIn v2.1 is available in larger (bulk) quantities at a discount. This might for a training event, by Integrated Alliances, by your organization or perhaps by someone else.

This is a great gift book for employees, customers and partners. They will thank you and remember you!

## Custom Versions and White Label Books

RockTheWorld with LinkedIn v2.1 is available in customized formats and as a "white-labeled" book. Put your company's branding on the cover, on the back page, inside the book or add additional material. We will make a custom version of the book just for you!

## Contact

In any of these cases, please contact us at 303-683-9600 or Training@IntegratedAlliances.com to discuss special book orders.

# Getting Help From Integrated Alliances and The LinkedIn Rockstars

RockTheWorld with LinkedIn v2.1 is an integral component in the Integrated Alliances LinkedIn and Social Selling programs and in our keynote addresses and breakout sessions.

1. Want to know more about the Integrated Alliances LinkedIn and Social Selling programs? Whether it's a 1-hour webinar (or webinar series), a 1-hour, 4-hour or day-long program, you will be SO HAPPY you brought Integrated Alliances in to get your team on track.

2. Need a rockin' keynote speaker that teaches AND entertains? Mike O'Neil, Lori Ruff (or Mike AND Lori) will have your crowd screaming for an encore as they turn your event into one that will never be forgotten.

3. Could you or your company sell more effectively using the services of Integrated Alliances and the LinkedIn Rockstars? Take a load off yourself and bring us in to help you. TOGETHER we can do amazing things to get your teams marketing and selling more effectively.

Please reach out at 303-683-9600 or Training@IntegratedAlliances.com.

21575523R00093

Made in the USA
San Bernardino, CA
27 May 2015